Quick-Start
SPANISH
SECOND EDITION

EVERYTHING YOU NEED TO KNOW BEFORE YOU START OR RESTART SPANISH

Arlene M. Jullie

McGraw·Hill

New York   Chicago   San Francisco   Lisbon   London   Madrid   Mexico City
Milan   New Delhi   San Juan   Seoul   Singapore   Sydney   Toronto

1 2 3 4 5 6 7 8 9 0   VLP/VLP   0 9 8 7 6 5

ISBN 0-07-145163-3
Library of Congress Control Number: 2004065599

Cover design by La Shae V. Ortiz
Cover illustration and interior illustrations copyright © Chris Reed
Interior design by Village Typographers, Inc.

McGraw-Hill books are available at special quantity discounts to use as premiums and sales promotions, or for use in corporate training programs. For more information, please write to the Director of Special Sales, Professional Publishing, McGraw-Hill, Two Penn Plaza, New York, NY 10121-2298. Or contact your local bookstore.

This book is printed on acid-free paper.

Contents

Introduction

How many times have you wished you could be one of "those" people who learns languages easily, or marveled at someone who speaks five or six languages? Do you ever feel as if you are stuck behind an invisible glass wall when you visit a foreign country, or the person to whom you are speaking in English suddenly turns to someone else and rattles away in what might as well be Martian?

This little manual is *not* intended to teach you Spanish. Instead, this book was written with the purpose of decoding or demystifying the Spanish language so that you will have access to secrets that can help you learn Spanish more easily. Just as the ancient Aztecs and Mayans had mysteries or codes that have needed to be deciphered over the centuries, the Spanish language also has "secrets" that may very well elude you. Unconcealing those secrets could be the key for you, and most English-speakers, to mastering another language, as well as giving you a quick-start in any Spanish class.

I own a television set with which I am fairly familiar, at least the front panel. If I were planning to watch the show of all times, and suddenly the TV began to make strange popping noises, I'd be upset, scared, and totally intimidated. I know that if I could remove the back panel, and if I knew the secrets behind the screen, so to speak, I would have no cause to be intimidated. But, I would not take a TV repair course because

    a. I never do things like that . . . other people do.

    b. Someone else I know can do it instead.

    c. I am too dumb, too old, too incompetent.

    d. It would take a lot of time, and I am very busy.

    e. I really don't have an ongoing use for learning that.

    f. I have never been good at those kinds of things.

All of these same reasons can be used by someone who would desperately like to be able to communicate in a foreign language. Go back over the six reasons, and see if you fit into any of these categories when it comes to learning Spanish.

In my 25 years of teaching and running my own language school, I have noticed that these reasons are the ones most people seem to have for not learning a new language. I also noticed recently that, like most American foreign language teachers, I have failed to tell my students the secrets of the language they were learning before they began, especially in the plain, easy, and fun English terms contained on the pages to follow.

This book is for people who are about to start a Spanish class, for everyone who has ever tried to learn Spanish, and for people who think they could never learn Spanish because they are too dumb, too old, or just plain incompetent. It's for business people, for upcoming junior high and high school students, for homemakers, for college students with a foreign language requirement, or for anyone who loves to travel to Spanish-speaking countries. It's for people who are scared silly to sign up for a Spanish class or for those who are actually taking a class and feel somewhat to completely lost.

Before You Start

Before you start you will need: a box of crayons, markers, or colored pencils; a pen or pencil; highlighter pens; a few magazines; several sheets of construction paper and plain white, unlined paper; a tape recorder; classical music tapes (a radio with an FM station will do); masking tape; a kush ball or any small ball (rubber ball, a tennis ball, golf ball, whatever you have at home); a package of M&M's or your favorite candy or cookies for treats; and . . . A HAT! **Assemble these now**, before you go on. You can wait on the hat.

Make a check mark below for each item or items you have assembled:

_____ a box of crayons, markers, or colored pencils

_____ a pen or pencil

_____ different-colored highlighter pens

_____ 5 sheets of colored construction paper

_____ 10 sheets of plain white, unlined paper

_____ a tape recorder or radio

_____ classical music tapes (unless you have a radio)

_____ masking tape

_____ a ball

_____ 2–3 magazines, preferably colorful magazines with food pictures

_____ treats (M&M's, cookies, fruit, whatever you love to eat)

If you are an adult, you may think that you can just skim through this book and learn without all the "kiddy stuff." NO! Your success is dependent upon this list. Become a kid and do it to get the most benefit.

Notes About How to Use This Playbook for Optimal Results

Scan

Scan the different parts of the book for three minutes. Using the colored pencils or markers, jot down words you noticed or that stood out. Use the space below.

Read

Read over the Contents if you haven't already done so. Notice that the book is divided into three sections. **Section One** will give you a quick-start in being able to impress your teacher and classmates because you can make the correct sounds in Spanish. **Section Two** will give you what you need to know about the structure of Spanish before your first day of class. **Section Three** will prepare you for the second quarter or semester and is ideal for someone who has studied Spanish before and wants a good review.

Draw and Color

Be sure to color all the pictures in this book, beginning right here. You can also highlight anything you feel is important and want to remember. Also, after you have finished each chapter, draw and color a personalized picture—a picture just you would identify with—next to each title in the Contents. For example, draw a bumblebee next to the chapter titled, " 'To Be' or Not 'To Be' " or three or four little houses next to the chapter called "De 'Burbs." This is not an art class. Don't worry if it doesn't look good. It's for your own use. Be creative! And, above all else, **have fun!**

Relax

Research shows that we learn much more easily when we are relaxed. Read over the following paragraph once or twice; then put on some soft, relaxing music; close your eyes; and go through all the activities, visualizing each detail, adding your own sights, sounds, and smells if you like. At the end, just sit quietly for a moment, then slowly open your eyes. You will be ready to begin a new chapter or section in the book. **Do this each time you start new material.**

Close your eyes and picture a beach, maybe a beach in Mexico. Listen to the waves; notice the blue sky, the blue water, and the white waves; feel the breeze blowing your hair. Walk along the beach picking up shells, feeling the soft sand under your bare feet. Let the sun relax you all over. Breathe deeply. Pretend you're sipping a cold beverage or eating an icy popsicle. Can you taste it? Now sit down on the sand and pick up a handful of wet sand, rub it between your fingers, then rinse off your hands in the crystal clear water. Lie back and watch the clouds drifting across the sky; listen for the cry of seagulls, the swishing of palm tree branches in the wind. Let your imagination bring you back to the place where you started, and when you are ready, slowly open your eyes.

You see, the mind doesn't know the difference between real and imagined, so you will get the same physical benefits as a short trip to the beach, but no sunburn!

Mind Maps

At the end of certain chapters you will be asked to draw a mind map or memory map of what you learned. Unlike an outline, a mind map is a picture with key points illustrated. The simplest is to draw a large circle or sun, with straight lines (rays) or spokes coming out from the center. Write in the key points you want to remember on the rays of the sun with different-colored pencils or markers. Here is a mind map about how to use this playbook.

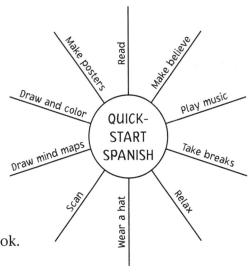

Music

As you read each chapter, listen to relaxing music. If you like classical music, either baroque ("The Four Seasons" by Vivaldi and Handel's "Water Music" are wonderful) or anything by Mozart is perfect. There are some places where you get to talk out loud. Use the music when you're doing this.

Make Believe

Let's pretend! Choose a new name for yourself in Spanish. This may seem totally silly, but try it anyway. Close your eyes and imagine that you ARE a Spanish-speaking person, even if your voice of reason tells you: "Cut it out!" What if you really could rattle off in Spanish like they do in South or Central America, Spain, and Mexico? Who would you be? Pablo? Carmen? Dolores? Alfonso? Rosita? Juanita? José? Carlos? Marcos? María?

And while you're at it, where do you come from? Nobody has to know you're doing this crazy exercise. Allow yourself to dream. Are you from Panama or Bolivia? Mexico or Chile? Spain or Colombia? There! You now have a new identity. If you want, you can go one step farther: you can pretend you're any profession, age, or even weight and body type you want. Did you say you're a muscular Spanish bullfighter named José? A Colombian rock singer? Or a curvy Bolivian waitress named Carmen? It's your secret! Do you want to give yourself a last name? Choose one: González, Romero, Díaz, Blanco, Rodríguez. Just so you don't forget, also write your new name, profession, and where you're from, in bright colors, on the front page of this book.

Now you can put on your special hat. If you don't have a hat yet, find or buy one that goes with your new identity. Each time you wear it, pretend you are that person and that you speak Spanish fluently. If you can find Mexican or Latin American or Spanish music, play it when you put on your hat and prepare for *Quick-Start Spanish*.

Draw a Picture

Use the space below to draw a picture of yourself in your new identity. What would you wear? What kind of car would you drive? Where do you live? Let your imagination run wild. When I am María Dolores González, the famous actress, I live in an ocean villa in Costa Rica and drive a white convertible sports car. I have a gorgeous tan body and wear miniskirts and a bikini top!

Me llamo _____
(Write your new name here.)

Me llamo literally means "I call myself." It is the most common way to introduce yourself in Spanish. Pronounce it like this: may **yah**-mo. Just say that a few times to get the feel of it rolling off your tongue. Close your eyes and see yourself in a park or a house in another country, introducing yourself to a boy or a girl, a man or a woman. (*Me llamo . . .*) Don't forget to smile!

Learning Environment

Prepare your learning environment next. Choose a special place to read this book that's just for Spanish. If you've been shopping in a Spanish-speaking country, put your blanket, maracas, castanets, or *sombrero* (hat) in your spot. Maybe add a vase with crepe paper or real flowers or plants. Make sure it's clean and inviting, a place you look forward to being in. Perhaps it's your favorite recliner or a beanbag chair. Some people prefer a table or desk. The environment should have nice vibes whether it's your porch, your balcony, or your bed. Have your materials nearby: tape player, boom box, radio, or Walkman; tapes of classical, Spanish, or relaxation music; your paper, crayons, or colored markers; and your HAT! Now, make a sign for your "Spanish Place" by including your new name on it, something like:

> Rosita's Spanish Corner
>
> José's Cantina (that's a bar in Spanish)
>
> Carmen's Cancún Beach Resort

Posters

Make a couple of bright, colorful, positive learning posters including pictures cut from magazines. Add captions such as "Spanish is a piece of cake," "I love Spanish," "Learning the secrets of Spanish is going to be as easy as pie," or "Spanish is easy and fun." Glue the pictures on the colored construction paper, and tape these to the walls around your space. You may think this is stupid or time-consuming. Believe me, you will learn more easily if you follow the instructions, even if it means getting up from where you are sitting reading this book and letting yourself get creative. Go ahead!

Breaks

- Spend no more than 15–30 minutes at a time with each section or chapter.
- Take a break and have a treat at the end of each study period.
- Review your favorite games, especially "The Lulu, Lola, Lalo Game" and the "Yoyo Exercise," after each break or before each new session.

Note: This entire book will take you from 10 to 15 hours to finish, depending on how much Spanish you already know and how much **fun** you allow yourself to have. For the first and second sections—recommended for before your first day of Spanish class—it should take you even less time!

Now you are ready for Section One.

OH SEE CAN YOU SAY?

There are six parts to Section One. This section will clue you in on how to *see* and *say* the sounds of the Spanish language. It is important to master each part. Take your time! Take a break between each part, and go back and review any time.

Now, it is time to meet Sofía, the famous anthropologist, who will be your personal guide to decoding the Spanish language.

Me llamo Sofía

PART ONE

De Bowels!
De Bowels Are Berry Berry Important!

The five most important sounds in the Spanish language are the bowels, that is, the vowels, excuse me! You see, *b*s and *v*s sound the same in Spanish.

> **a** = Open wide and say "**Ah!**"
> **e** = like the **ay*** sound as in *pay*
> **i** = has the English sound **ee** as in "My country 'tis of *thee*"
> **o** = **Oh!** Sounds like the *o* in *snow*
> **u** = It's Halloween. Say b**oo**!
> **y** = is often used like a vowel and sounds just like the Spanish letter *i* (**ee**)

*Sometimes *e* also sounds like the *e* in *met*. For example, The Spanish word *el* rhymes with the English word *bell,* and *es* rhymes with *Bess.* Practice both sounds.

Now, draw your own personalized picture or symbol next to each letter. Make it something you'll look at and remember. For example, mine would be:

A	E	I	O	U

Draw yours here:

A	E	I	O	U

Now, repeat the Spanish vowels as you look at your picture. Do this several times. Sing them to "Jingle Bells."

    AAA, AAA, AEIOU
    AAA, AAA, AEIOU
    AAA, AAA, AEIOU
    AAA, AAA, AEIOU!

Now, add a consonant (any letter that is not a vowel) before each vowel. Start with *n, m, p, s, t, l, f, d,* and sing the following sounds to "Jingle Bells":

na-na-na,   na-na-na,   na, ne, ni, no, nu
ma-ma-ma,   ma-ma-ma,   ma, me, mi, mo, mu
pa-pa-pa,   pa-pa-pa,   pa, pe, pi, po, pu
sa-sa-sa,   sa-sa-sa,   sa, se, si, so, su
ta-ta-ta,   ta-ta-ta,   ta, te, ti, to, tu
la-la-la,   la-la-la,   la, le, li, lo, lu
fa-fa-fa,   fa-fa-fa,   fa, fe, fi, fo, fu

da-da-da,   da-da-da,   da, de, di, do, du (Practith thith one with your tongue thticking out: tha, the, thi, tho, thu, like the *th* in **the, they, this**.)

That's how the *d* sounds in Spanish. Kind of soft and gentle.

Tricky Sounds

J   How do you say *José* and *Juan*, as in San José (California) and San Juan (Puerto Rico)? OK, so you know the letter *j* in Spanish sounds like an *h* in English.

Say: ja, je, ji, jo, ju

How do you spell "Ha, ha, ha!" (when someone laughs) in Spanish? *Ja, ja, ja!*

H   The letter *h* is just not pronounced at all in Spanish. It's as though it were invisible, unheard, unpronounced. You never, never hear it. Pretend it's not even there. A "hotel" sounds like *otel.* (Did you ever pass a hotel with a neon sign where the *h* was burned out?) Same for hospital: *ospital.*

So then, how do you say: ha, he, hi, ho, hu?

Just like *a, e, i, o, u*!

(If, as in English, an *h* has a *c* before it, you say *ch*, as in "cha cha cha.")

B and V   You know already that *b* and *v* both sound like *b*; in fact, the letter *v* is called "little *b*" in Spanish because the two letters sound so similar.

Now say: ba, be, bi, bo, bu; va, ve, vi, vo, vu

They should sound the same. (In some countries the *v* sounds a little like *w*.)

X   The letter *x* sounds just like our *x*, so *examen* ("exam"), *extra, excelente, excepto* are as easy to say in Spanish as they are in English. One *excepción* is the word *México*, which is pronounced **may**-hee-coh.

Note: If you travel to the Yucatan peninsula of Mexico, many Mayan words contain *x*s. They are pronounced *sh*: Xel-Ha, Xcaret, Xpu-Ha for example are pronounced shell-ha, shh-caret, shhpoo-ha. (Did you notice that in the Mayan language, you hear and say the *h* sound the same as in English?)

Y The letter *y* sounds like the *y* in *yes,* except when it stands alone or is the last letter of a word, in which case it has an **ee** sound, like the vowel *i.*

Say: ya, ye, yi, yo, yu

Say: *y* (Can you believe that *y* is a real word? It's the way you say "and" in Spanish.)

Z The letter *z* is always pronounced like an *s* in Spanish.

za, ze, zi, zo, zu
sa, se, si, so, su

Repeat these last two lines several times. They are identical.

P.S. If you go to Spain, you will notice that people seem to lisp a lot. It's because they pronounce their *z*s like *th.* So the metal ZINC would be pronounced THINK in Spain, and SINK in Spanish America! Zinck about zat!

 Take a break if you want to before the next part.

(PART TWO)

Oh Say, Can You See?

If you have taken a break after Part One, go back and review the vowel sounds. If you haven't taken a break, pretend you are a famous singer, vocalizing before you go on stage. Sing the same note, or go up and down the scale. Wave your arms around and belt it out: na, ne, ni, no, nu! ja, je, ji, jo, ju! ba, be, bi, bo, bu! ta, te, ti, to, tu! Keep going!

Now, stop, and read the following sentence out loud twice:

Ce, ci *Ce* and *ci* are pronounced **say** and **see** instead of "kay" and "key."

Remember the rule about spelling the word *receive* in English: *i before e except after c?*
OK, sing the following song to the tune of "The Star-Spangled Banner"!

Oh **say** can you **see**,
It's as easy as pie
That a C sounds like S
Before E, before I!
(*Here comes the high part* "and the rockets' red glare")
If it comes before U, before O, before A
The C sounds a lot like the small letter K
Oh **ce** can you **ci**, it's as easy as pie
That a C sounds like S, before E, before I.

Sing it one more time now that you have the hang of it. (You may sit down now!)

Now say: *Coca, cola, cucu, caca* (oops!). Then say: *cero, cafecito, cita, celos, cine.**
Just remember *ce* sounds like *say*, and *ci* sounds like *see*.

*Did you say: **say**-roh, cah-fay-**see**-toh, **see**-tah, **say**-los, **see**-nay? Good!

Repeat the vowels one more time: a, e, i, o, u; ca, **ce**, **ci**, co, cu

Q Another "k" sound is the letter *q*, which is pronounced *cu* as a letter of the
alphabet. *Q* is always, always, always followed by the letter *u* in Spanish.
Qu Qu Qu. The word *que* is pronounced **kay** and means either
"what" or "that," depending on the context.

> QUÉ = KAY = K
> OK! OK! OK!
> OH QUE! OH QUE! OH QUE!

So . . . if someone says something to you in Spanish and you want to ask "what?"
you can just say: *¿Qué?* Pretend someone just rattled something off in Spanish.
Open your eyes wide, look puzzled, and say: *¿Qué?* You can also say *¿Cómo?*, which
is more correct, even though it means "how?"

What? Just remember: Como is the name of a lake in Italy, and it also means
"how" or "what" in Spanish.

Read this sentence again out loud. Don't forget it!

Ge, gi You thought you were done with the national anthem, right? Wrong!
Because there is another letter, the letter *g*, that follows the same rule. Before
the letters *e* and *i*, the *g* is pronounced like an English letter *h*. So *ge* and *gi*
are pronounced **hay** and **hee**. An army general is a *hen*eral. So now, you can
sing that song again:

 Oh **hay**, can you **hee**, *(sounds pretty silly!)*
It's as easy as pie
That a G sounds like H
Before E, before I!
(Remember the high part comes next)
If it comes before A, before O, before U
The G sounds like *ga* or like *go* or like *goo*
Oh **ge** can you **gi**, it's as easy as pie
That a G sounds like H
Before E, before I!

A note to the curious: if you need to make the *g* sound, as in the English word *gate*, before an *e* or *i*, you must write a *u* after it. However, the *u* is silent! So *gue* and *gui* are pronounced **gay** or **geh** and **ghee**, not **gway** or **gweh** and **gwee**. Now pronounce these words: *gema, gelatina, generoso, giro, gimnasia*; how about *guerra, guerrilla, guiso, guía*? Did the first five words sound like **hay** and **hee**? Did the last four words sound like **geh** and **ghee**? Genius!

(PART THREE)

Bonbons, Benders, Green Beans, Bones, and Baboons

When you add the letter *n* **after** each of the vowels *a, e, i, o, u,* they sound like this:

> *an* sounds like **on**, as in *bonbon*
> *en* sounds like the letter *n* or like the *en* in *bender* (or *pen*)
> *in* sounds like **een** or **ean**, as in *green bean*
> *on* sounds like **own** or **one**, as in *bone*
> *un* sounds like **oon**, as in *baboon*

So just say: **bon**bon, **ben**der, **bean**, **bone**, ba**boon**. Say them again!

Now try: *an, en, in, on, un* in Spanish. They should rhyme with the words above them! Do they?

How about *ban, ben, bin, bon, bun*? And *van, ven, vin, von, vun* are identical!

Under each syllable below, draw a picture of something that rhymes with each sound. If you're like I am and couldn't draw a baboon if your life depended on it, try a cartoon or a loon!

AN   EN   IN   ON   UN

(PART FOUR)

Bathing Suits or Sandals?

Here is a word about diphthongs: (Say what? Diph-thongs?)

OK, if you don't know what a diphthong is, choose one of the following definitions:

   a. A narrow strap worn as a bathing suit on the beaches of South America

   b. Sandal-like shoes, usually made in Southeast Asia

   c. A combination of any two vowels to form a single syllable

C is the correct answer! Here are seven of the thirteen most-used diphthongs in Spanish:

ai / ay = sounds like the letter *i* in *hi!* When you hit your thumb with a hammer, you yell out *¡Ay!,* not "Ow!" if you speak Spanish.

ei / ey = sounds like the **ay** in *say.* The sport *béisbol* (**bayss**-bohl) sounds almost the same as it does in English.

oi / oy = sounds like the **oy** in *boy.*

au = sounds like the **ow** in *wow.*

ua = sounds like the **wa** in *water.* In fact, *agua* (**ah**-gwah) means "water" in Spanish.

ue = sounds like **way**. As in "No ue, José!"

uo = sounds like **wo** as in "***Wo*e** is me!"

Go through the seven diphthongs one more time, except throw your kush ball or tennis ball up in the air each time you say one. Do it again!

Extra Letters

Is that enough about bowels and vowels (which you now know are pronounced the same)? Just a few more points on pronunciation. First, there is an extra letter in the Spanish alphabet. Yep, that's right. A letter we don't have in English. It looks like this: *ñ*. There are also some letter combinations, or blends, that have distinct sounds: *ch, ll, rr.*

ñ = sounds like **ni** as in *onion* or **ny** as in *canyon*. Ever hear of *mañana* ("tomorrow")?

ch = sounds like **ch** as in *church* or *cha-cha*.

ll = is pronounced like the English letter *y*, so a *llama* sounds like **yah**-mah.*

rr = is a trilled sound, like a motorcycle engine revving up. Try it!

*Remember *me llamo* ("my name is/I call myself")? It's the same sound. In some countries, Argentina, for example, that sound is more like a *j*, like the movie *Dr. Zhivago*; or you may hear the *ll* in Mexico said like the *j* in the English word *pajama*.

Want to try saying *me llamo* with these two new sounds? Go ahead!

(PART FIVE)

Squashed Bugs

Have you ever noticed how foreign words seem to have little marks over the letters? Those are squashed bugs! No, actually they are *accent marks*. There are two marks you need to know in Spanish. They look like this: ´ and ˜. One goes over the vowels *a, e, i, o, u*, like this *á, é, í, ó, ú*. It shows that you should *emphasize* or *stress* that letter. Like *café, papá, París, calicó, cucú* ("cuckoo" in English). It is officially an accent mark. The other, which only looks like an accent, but is not considered one, is a *tilde* as in "Waltzing Ma-tilde," and it is only found above the letter *n*, like this: *ñ*. Say: I put onions on my bunions. Now say: I put oñons on my buñons. Get the picture?

By the way, do you like *piña coladas*? *Piña* is the Spanish word for "pineapple."

In the space below draw a BIG pineapple! Make sure to color it. Then, inside the pineapple, write everything you learned so far in Section One, or the most important things you remember. You'll have a mind map for future reference!

Take a break before going on to the games in Part Six.

Games and Exercises

The Lulu, Lola, Lalo Game

All words in Spanish, or any language, are made up of syllables. Syllables are the way we divide up words: *mon-key, so-fa, te-le-vi-sion*. In the English word *monkey*, **mon** is the first syllable, and **key** is the second syllable. There are hundreds of words in Spanish that have only two syllables. In the Spanish word *mono*, which means "monkey," the first syllable is **mo**, and the second is **no**.

In this exercise you will practice the sounds you have learned so far, which will make it super easy to say the short Spanish words you will learn in the exercise that follows this one.

Rules of the game   Make up at least 25 crazy words using two or three of these syllables. Say these out loud and practice the Spanish vowels! Or, if you like, write them in the margins before you say them aloud. For example: *poba, gobe, meta, niva* . . . you may unknowingly say a real word in Spanish!

Fill in the seven blank spaces, placed randomly in the chart, with your own made-up syllables. You can make a syllable with a letter (consonant) followed by a vowel. Don't forget the extras: *ch, ll, ñ, rr.*

me	te	jo*	pe	lo	ma	si
pa	li	ve*	se	ba	cha	ci*
le	so	fe	la	chi	da	yi
vu*	na	mi	ye	va*	ti	lli*
ta	lla*	po	da	ca	lle	hi*
ya	be	che	yu		gi*	ñe*
di	ña	ze*	pu		ja*	de
mo	ho*	sa	so	fo	llo	mu
je*	yo	va*		ve*	lo	
ce*	to	lu	ho*	tu		me
ni	cho	ge*	bi	llu*	yo	co
vo*	fa	ño*		ju*	go	ji*
pi	ga	zi*	ne	ri	bo	
chu	bu	za*	gu	cu	ñi*	ja*

*These are tricky syllables. You may want to jot down their pronunciation rules in the margin.

The Yoyo Exercise

Would you be surprised to know that the word for yoyo in Spanish is also *yoyo*? Most of the words below have two syllables, and all of them have a meaning, so now you are not only practicing the sounds you have learned so far, but also saying real Spanish words that you will surely encounter when you take a Spanish class. If you want to know what these words mean, turn to the Appendix at the back of this book. To make the exercise more fun, repeat the words in a singsong voice and move your head up and down or side to side, like a yoyo! Accent the first syllable if the word has two syllables, and stress the second-to-the-last syllable if it has three. Example: **mo**-no, **pi**-so, za-**pa**-to, pe-**pi**-no.

mono	casi	gato	hola
piso	foca	foto	tuna
pisa	peso	pozo	gafas
niño	tina	pato	cuna
paso	payaso	llega	pata
sapo	mano	año	hoja
oso	osa	usa	noche
palo	lima	sopa	hilo
buzo	mozo	barco	paleta
vino	casa	malo	buho
ojo	cada	nada	papa
foco	tope	pepino	toca
zapato	cola	pavo	piña
poco	loco	Paco	ola
come	solo	taza	seda
jugo	cita	mapa	puma
sala	laguna	mala	pollo
pelo	chula	sello	cucú
saco	mesa	sino	mina
tonto	cine	luna	jota
gata	mamá	papá	hijo
humo	plato	dedo	hija
hora	días	lunes	masa
gorro	vaca	bata	sano
carne	leña	vida	primo

The Better Body Exercise

This fun-filled exercise is great practice for people who claim they cannot roll their *rs*.

Directions   Read the following words as fast as you can, and believe it or not, by the end, you'll be rolling your *rs* like a regular Spanish speaker!

better body   better body   better body
pretty pretty   pretty birdie   pretty birdie
potty potty   little potty   little bitty potty
pretty little birdie bought a pretty little potty
toddy Teddy   Teddy tooty   tooty Fruity
pot o' tea   pot o' tea   pot o' tea
buddy buddy   muddy muddy   muddy buddy
Eddy Eddy   Paddy Paddy   Daddy Daddy
pedal pedal piddle piddle piddle diddle
daddle daddle dawdle   oughta dawdle oughta dawdle
paddle paddle   potta potta   petty petty
body body   beddy beddy beady beady   bootie bootie

Repeat the whole exercise three times, going faster and faster all the time, until you sound like a motorcycle!

The problem with rolling an *r* is not that you are incapable of making the sound, it's that you have to think *ddddd* or *ttttt* instead of *r*.

The Bera Bari Exercise

Here's where the rubber hits the road. We will now do this exercise in Spanish!

Directions   Read the words in the first line in English, just as you did in the previous exercise, then read the line below it in Spanish *exactly the same way*. No deviations, no detours! The sounds are identical.

Body body body
Bari   bari   bari   (remember, it's **not** an *r* sound—force yourself to say *ddd*)

Betty Betty bootie bootie
Beri   beri   buri   buri

Etta Etta Eddy Eddy oughta oughta
Era era eri   eri   ora   hora

Notty netty needy naughty nootie
Nari   neri   niri   nori   nuri

Potty petty peedy pawdie pootie
Pari   peri   piri   pori   puri

Dotty detti Deedee dawty duty
Dari   deri   diri   dori   duri

You can go through more letters from the alphabet if you like, using different consonants (*f, l, m, s, t, v*) followed by a Spanish vowel like you did in "Jingle Bells" (na, ne, ni, no, nu), and adding the letter *r*. But don't say the American *r* sound; use the *ddd* or *ttt* sound instead. Here's an example:

English: Faddy feddy feedie fawty foodie
Spanish: fari   feri   firi   fori   furi

English: Lahdi leddi leedie lawdy loodie   (You're on your own now.)
Spanish:

English: M
Spanish:

English: S
Spanish:

English: T
Spanish:

English: V
Spanish:

Here are some possible ways of spelling the mostly nonsense English words followed by the Spanish sounds:

Moddy metti meaty maughty mootie
mari   meri   miri   mori   muri

Sotty setty seaty saughty suitie
sari   seri   siri   sori   suri

Toddy teddy teady tawdie tootie
tari   teri   tiri   tori   turi

Voddy veddy veadie vaudy voody
vari   veri   viri   vori   vuri

The big see and say exam   Delight your family and impress your friends by pronouncing the name of this small village in Mexico:

PARANGARICUTIRIMICUARO
pot-on-goddy-coo-teedy-<u>mee</u>-cua-doh

Break it into syllables: Pa-ran-ga-ri-cu-ti-ri-**mi**-cua-ro!! (accent **mi**)

Now say it three times as fast as you can!

If you still haven't taken a break, this is the time. Have a treat, maybe a pot o' tea, some chips and salsa, or some *cho-co-la-tes*.

The "What Am I?" Game

You should play this game **after you have had a break.**

Did you realize that you ALREADY KNOW more than 4,000 words in Spanish? That's because many words we have in English came from Latin, as did words in Spanish, French, Italian, and Portuguese.

Directions Now that you have been practicing how to pronounce Spanish words, read through the lists below **three times.** Believe it or not, you will say and understand 220 words in Spanish, which are just a fraction of all the words that are similar to words we have in English! The term for words that are similar to words in our own language is *cognates.*

1. The first time, just read them to yourself to recognize them. You may have to take off a final *e* or *a* or *o*, or even the last two letters to have it look like English.

2. The second time, circle the syllable that should be **stressed** according to the following rules:

   a. If a word ends in a vowel (*a, e, i, o, u, y*) or *n* or *s*, circle the next-to-last syllable.

   b. If it ends in a consonant other than *n* or *s*, circle the last syllable.

   c. If it has an accent mark (squashed bug), circle the syllable with the accent. For example: fa-(ná)-ti-co; (dó)-lar; ca-(fé); chacha(chá).

3. The third time, read the words out loud with the Spanish pronunciation, stressing the circled syllable. (The answers are in the Appendix!)

ac-tor	sen-si-ble	in-te-li-gen-te	ra-dio
te-le-vi-sión	po-si-ble	pro-ba-ble	a-ni-mal
dó-lar	co-mer-cial	e-le-gan-te	e-le-fan-te
to-ma-te	im-por-tan-te	ta-xi	i-lu-sión
ar-ti-fi-cial	co-lor	ba-na-na	mos-qui-to
mo-tor	na-tu-ral	o-pi-nión	po-pu-lar
tro-pi-cal	pia-no	ac-ci-den-te	am-bu-lan-cia
as-pi-ri-na	mú-si-ca	pro-fe-sor	res-tau-ran-te
ho-tel	sec-tor	ti-gre	ca-fé
sa-xo-fón	fru-ta	ga-so-li-na	im-po-si-ble
ge-ne-ral	e-le-men-to	e-fec-to	per-so-na
ci-vil	de-ci-sión	in-fe-rior	su-pe-rior
do-cu-men-to	die-ta	com-ple-to	a-pe-ti-to
bi-ci-cle-ta	ham-bur-gue-sa	cri-mi-nal	di-fe-ren-te
pro-ble-ma	ba-llet	mu-si-cal	den-tal
mon-ta-ña	far-ma-cia	ne-gro	as-tro-nau-ta
gui-ta-rra	fút-bol	te-nis	golf
pro-gra-ma	sand-wich	li-mo-na-da	u-sual

i-le-gal	or-di-na-rio	nor-mal	se-cre-ta-ria
i-ni-cial	au-to	mo-der-no	tra-di-cio-nal
de-mó-cra-ta	pre-si-den-te	car-pin-te-ro	ca-len-da-rio
co-rrec-to	fa-ná-ti-co	cha-cha-chá	fo-to
dic-cio-na-rio	a-me-ri-ca-no	tu-ris-ta	ta-co
mo-men-to	te-lé-fo-no	ex-cur-sión	in-ven-tor
doc-tor	den-tis-ta	vol-cán	au-to-bús
len-gua-je	es-truc-tu-ra	e-fec-ti-vo	

Stop! Instead of reading to yourself or circling, just say the next words aloud. The meanings are easy to figure out. Remember the endings sound like *-eesta*.

activista	analista	artista	ciclista
capitalista	fatalista	idealista	pesimista
motorista	naturalista	novelista	oculista
conformista	dentista	economista	especialista
protagonista	realista	reformista	socialista
violinista	guitarrista	pianista	taxista (taxi driver)

Many words ending in *-tion* in English end in *-ción* in Spanish. Make sure you pronounce *-ción* like *see-own* and not *shun*. And stress or accent the **-ción**.

conversación	nación	condición	emoción
porción	ración	invitación	información
ambición	acción	moción	imaginación
corporación	exportación	ilustración	aplicación
admiración	edición	obligación	interpretación
función	intuición	adaptación	mención
aviación	colección	detección	construcción
educación	corrección	distracción	comunicación
decoración	apreciación	recepción	destrucción

Many words that end in *-ty* in English end in *-dad* or *-idad* in Spanish. Can you tell what these words mean? Accent the **-dad**.

posibilidad	necesidad	comunidad	realidad
calamidad	fraternidad	autoridad	flexibilidad
capacidad	agilidad	velocidad	humanidad
universidad	claridad	facilidad	caridad (charity)

Want to try a few more? You may need to go back to circling for the correct pronunciation. If in doubt about the meaning, try the word without the first or last letter. For example, *espacio* = space, *calmo* = calm, *esquí* = ski.

espacio	escorpión	religioso	liberal
computadora	sentimental	romántico	famoso
banco	dinamita	fabuloso	cuestión

sinfonía	ginecología	raro	especial
delicioso	cristal	positivo	negativo
análisis	misterio	misterioso	curioso
maravilloso	rápido	precioso	religión
protestante	católico	pirámide	ruina
dinámico	monstruo	estúpido	programa
calmo	clásico	fantástico	esquí

Check the Appendix in case you want to make sure of the meanings and correct pronunciation of these words.

The "Oh Solo Mio" Game

Rules of the game   Go through all the words on the preceding pages, not SAYING or READING but **SINGING** the words. Pretend you are a famous singer. Do you have a microphone? If not, use a magic marker, and SING into it. Put on some opera, rock, country, or your favorite music that is instrumental, and read these familiar words to music! **This is an important exercise!** Like sit-ups, doing these exercises will pay off, even if you don't want to do them. The next time you are in a Mexican restaurant, in the Spanish-speaking part of town, or visiting a Spanish-speaking country, you'll be able to pronounce menus, signs, and billboards with ease!

Finished? It's time for a break again. Good work! **¡Fantástico!**

BARE BONES

Did you ever sing the song about how "the foot bone's connected to the ankle bone, and the ankle bone's connected to the shin bone"? Well, this section will teach you the bare bones of the Spanish language. Even though you can't see your bones, they're hidden under your skin, right? Well, this is your chance to find out what's hidden under the surface of Spanish. A three-year-old Mexican or Uruguayan child can speak Spanish well, but he or she isn't aware of the "bare bones" that you'll be discovering in this section.

1

Sex

(All about the bird and the bee, the birds and the bees)

UNO

Begin with the relaxation exercise in the introduction, or do some deep, slow breathing with your eyes closed. Next, drink a glass of water: you will be feeding your brain! If it's been a while since you completed Section One, go back and do one of the three exercises at the end of that section for a pronunciation review. Are you wearing your sombrero *(hat)? Is the relaxing music playing?*

Now you are ready to talk about SEX!

 If you've ever been to a Spanish-speaking country, or met visitors from one, particularly people from a big city, you've probably noticed the very feminine-looking women: lots of makeup and jewelry, long painted fingernails, dressed like fashion models; and the very masculine men: mustaches, dark hair, macho, handsome, sunglasses. Their language is the same way. EVERY SINGLE PERSON, PLACE, OR THING in Spanish, without exception, is either feminine or masculine—even trees and stones, bugs and snow, bicycles and bedspreads, floors and vacuum cleaners, even garbage. Really! Even a grain of sand. Even words like *love, hate, disappointment, joy, luck,* and *happiness.*

People, places, and things are all called *nouns.* The names of people or places, such as a city or country, are *proper nouns.* You've undoubtedly heard of them—Jane, John, Julie, Jakarta, New Jersey, and so on—and they are always capitalized. All the others, the noncapitalized ones, are called *common nouns.*

Apples and Bananas

In English if we see a picture of an apple, we usually just say, "apple," but in Spanish they say, "the apple." In English we say, "I like apples." In Spanish they say, "I like the apples." In English we say, "Water is wet." In Spanish they say, "The

water is wet." We say, "Bananas are yellow"; they say, "The bananas are yellow."
So how do you say in Spanish "Roses are red, violets are blue, sugar is sweet"?
That's right: "The roses are red, the violets are blue, the sugar is sweet!"

Don't Forget the *The*!

The sentences on the left are what we say in English. By adding *the*, how would
you say them in Spanish? Fill in the blanks:

Cats are furry. _____

Dogs chew bones. _____

Babies sleep all the time. _____

I love roses. _____

Strawberries are red and sweet. _____

Lions and elephants live in the jungle. _____

_____

I like vacations in Mexico! _____

People who talk too much wear me out. _____

_____

➡ *Answers are printed at the end of this chapter.*

How Do You Know Which Noun Is Which Sex?

In Spanish, you can tell a noun is feminine if it has the word *la* or *una* in front
of it. *La rosa, la banana* = the rose, the banana; *una rosa, una banana* = a rose,
a banana.

La and *una* are *articles*. Feminine articles. *La* is a definite article (*the*), and *una* is
an indefinite article (*a* or *an*). Can you see how *the* is more "definite" than *a* or *an*?

You can also tell a noun is masculine if it has the word *el* or *un*
(remember the sound in *baboon* or *babun*?) in front of it. For
example, *el café, el apartamento, el actor, el sofá* = the coffee, the
apartment, the actor, the sofa. *Un café, un apartamento, un actor,
un sofá* = a coffee, an apartment, an actor, a sofa.

El and *un* are also called *articles*. Masculine articles. *El* is the
definite article (*the*) and *un* is the indefinite article (*a* or *an*).

So, the definite articles are *la*, *el*. The indefinite articles are **una**, **un**.

Usually words ending in **-a** are feminine, as in the girls' names Rosita, Carmelita, Conchita, Juanita, Anita, María, and so on. Usually words ending in **-o** are masculine, as in the boys' names Antonio, Marco, Diego, Eduardo, Alberto, and Pablo. But there are exceptions (such as *un sofá*), and there are lots of Spanish nouns that don't end in either **-a** or **-o**. So, when you are learning the names of things in Spanish, it's worth trying to remember them with the correct definite or indefinite article in front.

Joke Time!

A little boy (*un muchacho*) once asked his grandma (*la abuela*), "How old are you, Grandma?" She answered, "You're not supposed to ask old people that question." A few minutes later he came back again and asked, "Grandma, how much do you weigh?" Again she answered, "You're not supposed to ask old people that question." A little later the *abuela* heard a crash, and the little *muchacho* ran in and exclaimed, "Grandma, your purse just fell off the table and I saw your driver's license, and I know how old you are, how much you weigh, and that you got an *F* in sex!"

That's why this chapter is called "Sex." It's really about *gender,* which is the technical term for what we've been talking about. All nouns in Spanish have a gender, either masculine or feminine.

More than One Bird or Bee

When there is more than one bird or one bee, you call them *the birds* and *the bees.* Both in English and in Spanish you just have to add an **-s** to make a word plural (more than one) instead of singular (just one). But first the article also has to change into the plural—*la* becomes **las**—so you say *las rosas* and *las bananas.* *El* becomes **los**, so you say *los apartamentos* and *los sofás.* It's the same for **una** and **un**. They become **unas** and **unos**.

In English, the plural of "a" is "some": *a hat, some hats.* In Spanish, you would say *un sombrero, unos sombreros* or *una rosa, unas rosas.* Can you see how "some roses" is more indefinite than "the roses"?

The technical word for singular and plural is *number.* Can you see why? Because there are a number of birds, bananas, apartments, not only one!

Note: If a noun doesn't end in **-o** or **-a**, just add **-es** to make it plural. *El animal* becomes *los animales. El actor* becomes *los actores.* So what is the plural of *el volcán, el autobús,* and *el pastor*?

➡ *The answer is at the end of the chapter.*

Game: Guess Which Sex I Am

Draw two big houses in the space below and label them the "EL, UN" house and the "LA, UNA" house. Now look at the nouns listed at the bottom of the page. Which house would each noun belong in? Write the correct noun inside your house. When you are finished, say the noun with the correct article. For example: *el pato* or *un pato*.

Pato, amigo, rosa, hoja (pronounced **oh**-hah), manzana, carro, sombrero, casa, cola, rana, hilo, luna, oso, foca, cuna, buzo, gato, muchacha, muchacho, niño, niña.

❥ *See the end of the chapter for the answers as well as the meanings of the words.*

In the space below, draw a "sun" mind map for everything you learned in this chapter. First make a big, big circle. Then draw spokes or lines coming out from the center. Fill in the lines with everything you remember. It's *not* cheating to go back and look! Finally, color the sun a bright color.

 Now go back and draw a picture about this chapter in the Contents!

Answers to "Don't Forget the *The*!"

The cats are furry. The dogs chew the bones. The babies sleep all the time. I love the roses. The strawberries are red and sweet. The lions and the elephants live in the jungle. I like the vacations in Mexico! The people who talk too much wear me out.

Answers to "More than One Bird or Bee"

Los volcanes, los autobuses, los pastores. *Volcanes* are volcanoes, *autobuses* are buses, and *pastores* are shepherds or pastors (ministers).

Answers to "Guess Which Sex I Am"

EL, UN	LA, UNA
pato, amigo, carro, sombrero, hilo, oso, buzo, gato, muchacho, niño	rosa, hoja, manzana, casa, cola, rana, luna, foca, cuna, muchacha, niña

Meanings of list of nouns in the order of the original exercise

duck, friend, rose, leaf, apple, car, hat, house, tail, frog, thread, moon, bear, seal, crib, skin diver, cat, girl, boy, child (boy), child (girl)

2

Color Me Blue

*Play some fun, lively classical music here. This is a short, easy chapter.
You will need your crayons or markers.*

In the space below, draw two stick figures holding hands, one labeled *noun,*
one labeled *adjective.*

Color this picture. The sky is blue, the
grass is green, my car is new, the tree is
tall, my house is big, and the sun is hot.

Blue, green, new, tall, big, hot—these
are called *descriptive adjectives.* Here's
a simple way to identify a descriptive
adjective. Can you say *too, more,* or
very before the word? Or can you add

-*er* to the end? If you can, you know it's a descriptive adjective. Try that with the
six adjectives at the beginning of this paragraph. It works, right? Adjectives always
go hand in hand with a noun (persons, places, and things).

About Chameleons

In English, adjectives never change their spelling, but in Spanish they change
like a chameleon changes color with a tree or plant. Adjectives change in *gender*
and *number.* If the noun is feminine, they turn feminine; if the noun is masculine,
they turn masculine; and if the noun is plural, they turn plural.

Here's how that would look: a *muchacho* is a boy, and a *muchacha* is a girl. If you wanted to say the boy is Mexican, you would describe him as *mexicano*. If the girl is Mexican, she would be *mexicana*. The boys would be *mexicanos*; the girls would be *mexicanas*. Remember to make the Spanish *x* sound like an English *h*, may-hee-**cah**-no.

Here's another surprise for you! In Spanish you never say:

new car	you say	car new
blue sky	you say	sky blue
green grass	you say	grass green
tall tree	you say	tree tall

So how do you say:

hot sun _____   thin man _____

old woman _____   large dog _____

purple blouse _____   fluffy cat _____

smart father _____   loving mother _____

crazy neighbor _____ small book _____

foolish person _____ pretty flower _____

handsome brother _____ long hair _____

➧ *See the end of the chapter for the correct answers.*

The Backwards Game

Draw and color ten things (nouns) with an adjective describing each one. Underneath write, in English, how you would say each one as if it were in Spanish.

The Chameleon Game I

Below, on the left is a list of nouns in Spanish from the "What Am I?" game in Section One (see page 15). On the right is a list of chameleon-like adjectives in Spanish. Draw a line from a noun in the left column to an adjective in the right column. Make them agree, like this:

Noun—Adjective

masculine singular—masculine singular

feminine singular—feminine singular

masculine plural—masculine plural

feminine plural—feminine plural

For example: *el doctor famoso.* You can use adjectives from the right column more than once!

El doctor	deliciosa
	delicioso
Los actores	famoso
	famosa
La bicicleta	famosos
	famosas
La limonada	fantástico
	fantásticos
El taco	fabulosa
	fantástica
La hamburguesa	deliciosos
	deliciosas
Las farmacias	importante
	importantes
El actor	excelente
	excelentes

➥ *Check possible answers at the end of the chapter.*

The Chameleon Game II

Under each picture write in Spanish what you see, using the following nouns and adjectives:

Nouns: muchacha, doctor, taco, hamburguesa, café
Adjectives: mexicano, americano, excelente, famoso, delicioso

Watch out for agreement! (The chameleon adjective changes color!)

➡ *The correct answers are at the end of the chapter.*

 Don't forget to go back and draw a picture in the Contents next to the name of this chapter.

It's time for a break!

Answers to "So how do you say" exercise

sun hot	man thin
woman old	dog large
blouse purple	cat fluffy
father smart	mother loving
neighbor crazy	book small
person foolish	flower pretty
brother handsome	hair long

Possible answers to "The Chameleon Game I"

Doctor-famoso (fantástico-excelente); Actor-fantástico (famoso-excelente); Bicicleta-fantástica (excelente); Limonada-deliciosa (excelente); Taco-delicioso (fantástico); Hamburguesa-fantástica (deliciosa); Farmacias-importantes (fantásticas-excelentes-famosas); Actores-famosos (importantes-excelentes)

Possible answers to "The Chameleon Game II"

muchachas mexicanas; hamburguesas deliciosas; taco excelente/delicioso; cafés deliciosos/excelentes; doctor famoso/excelente; muchacha americana

3

Me Too, Sue!

TRES

Think of three things about yourself that are wonderful. DON'T read on until you have done this! Say them out loud. You may now proceed.

Have you ever been around a little kid who is just learning to share?

"**My** truck!"
"No, that's your **sister's** truck."
"**My** cookie."
"No, you already ate **your** cookie; that is **his** cookie."

Little kids are possessive. People who are older than toddlers are possessive too, of their belongings, their cars, their clothes, or even of other people. *My, your, his, her, our,* and *their* are possessive adjectives. They show to whom something belongs.

If you remember from the preceding chapter, an adjective goes hand in hand with a noun. But in Spanish instead of going after the noun, as in *tree tall*, possessive adjectives go before the noun, the same as in English: *my truck, your cookie, his car, her husband, our cake, their house.* In Spanish they're so easy, it's a piece of cake! All you need to remember is "**Me too, Sue!**"

Mi (pronounced **me** in English) = "my."

mi casa = my house
mi chocolate = my chocolate
mi café = my coffee
mi sombrero = my hat
mi sofá = my sofa
mi carro = my car

Tu (pronounced like the word *too*) is used with your best friend, sister, relative, or someone you feel close to = "your."

tu casa = your house

tu chocolate = your chocolate (Now write in the rest, same as above)

_____

_____

_____

_____

Su (pronounced **sue**) is used for "your" with people you respect, people you don't know very well, or strangers. It also means "his," "her," and "their"!

su casa = your house, his house, her house, their house

su chocolate = _____

su café = _____

su sombrero = _____

su sofá = _____

su carro = _____

➥ *Answers are at the end of the chapter.*

One more thing: It doesn't matter if you are a male or a female, or whether what you're talking about is masculine or feminine, it's still always:

mi tu su   "Me too, Sue!"

More than One

If you have more than one house, chocolate, hat, sofa, or car, you simply say:

mis tus sus (**Meess, tooss, sooss**).

Write here how you would say the following, using *mis, tus, sus*:

My houses: _____

My chocolates: _____

Your cars: _____

Your hats: _____

His sofas: _____

Their houses: _____

➥ *Answers are at the end of the chapter.*

No Apostrophe *S*

In Spanish there is no *'s* (apostrophe *s*) to show that something belongs to someone. Instead, you use the word *de* (pronounced **day**), which means "of." So Juan's house is "the house of Juan," *la casa de Juan*; my father's house is "the house of my father," *la casa de mi papá*; my friend's chocolate is "the chocolate of my friend," *el chocolate de mi amigo*.

Also, in English we tend to slap words together to make things simple, like *hotel key, garage door, airplane ticket, convention center, metal table,* but in Spanish, guess what you say? If you guessed *the key of the hotel, the door of the garage, the ticket of the airplane, the center of conventions, the table of metal,* you are absolutely right. (Words that describe what something is made of—metal, cardboard, plastic, leather, gold, silver, etc.—don't need to be preceded by "the.") When you are in Cancún and see a sign for the CENTRO DE CONVENCIONES, you'll recognize it next time!

P.S. If you are really, really curious about how to say *our,* which was left out intentionally in order to make this not too complicated, it's *nuestro, nuestra, nuestros, nuestras.* It looks a little like the Cosa Nostra (the Mafia group meaning "our thing") and the Pater Noster (the Latin version of the prayer Our Father).

Game: Forget the Apostrophe!

How would you say the following if English were Spanish?

my mother's purse _____

your friend's car _____

his father's mustache _____

Mary's bicycle _____

John's bubble gum _____

car door _____

house key _____

cardboard box _____

leather shoes _____

boarding pass _____

➡ *Answers are at the end of this chapter.*

It's My Life

In the space below, draw a big picture of you and a group of your friends or family. You could be at work, at a party, at the beach, in school, wherever. When you are finished, draw arrows pointing to words that in English would take an apostrophe, such as "my dad's bathing suit," or "my friend's car." Label each thing as if you were writing it in Spanish: "the bathing suit of my dad," "the car of my friend," etc. Try to see if you can come up with at least ten items to label. Body parts count too!

The Suitcase Game

Draw a suitcase (a suitcase BIG!) in the space below, and inside it draw the following items (they are in Spanish, but you should be able to figure out what they mean). Check the answers at the end of the chapter if necessary.

shorts	blusa	jersey	pantalones	jeans
tenis	sombrero	disco	videocasete	pasta dental
aspirina	chocolate	sandalias	pijama	crema

Instructions You and two friends are taking a trip to Cancún together and have decided to share a suitcase. One friend is with you in the hotel room; the other one is already out on the beach. You are now unpacking the suitcase and sorting out what item belongs to whom and decide to say this in Spanish. What is *mi* or *mis,* what is *tu* or *tus,* and what is *su* or *sus?* **Remember, if the article of clothing ends in *s* you must use *mis, tus,* or *sus.***

➡ *Possible answers are at the end of the chapter.*

It's time for a break again! Just stand up and do jumping jacks, or touch your head, shoulders, knees, and toes five times before going on. If you know the tune to the song "Head and shoulders, knees and toes," you can sing the following in Spanish to the same tune: "Cabeza, hombros, piernas, pies." Don't pronounce the *h* in *hombros. Piernas, pies* actually mean "legs, feet." They are pronounced: **pyer**-nahs, **pyays.**

  Did you remember to go back and draw a picture in the Contents next to this chapter?

Answers for *tu* exercise

tu café
tu sombrero
tu sofá
tu carro

Answers for *su* exercise

your chocolate, his chocolate, her chocolate, their chocolate
your coffee, his coffee, her coffee, their coffee
your hat, his hat, her hat, their hat
your sofa, his sofa, her sofa, their sofa
your car, his car, her car, their car

Answers to "More than One"

mis casas
mis chocolates
tus (sus) carros
tus (sus) sombreros
sus sofás
sus casas

Answers to "Forget the Apostrophe!"

the purse of my mother
the car of your friend
the mustache of his father
the bicycle of Mary
the bubble gum of John
the door of the car
the key of the house
the box of cardboard
the shoes of leather
the pass of boarding

Possible answers to "The Suitcase Game"

Translation of items in suitcase:

shorts	blouse	jersey	pants	jeans
tennis shoes	hat	record	videocassette	toothpaste
aspirin	chocolate	sandals	pajamas	cream

MI, MIS	**TU, TUS**	**SU, SUS**
mis shorts, mis pantalones	tu jersey, tu blusa	sus jeans, su blusa
mis tenis, mi disco	tu videocasete	sus sandalias, su crema
mi pasta dental	tu aspirina	su pijama, su sombrero
mi chocolate		

Hugging and Kissing

CUATRO

Before you go on, look at the Spanish word for the number four in the chapter heading. Can you find a diphthong? Underline it now! How do you pronounce it?

(It's *ua*, pronounced **wa**.)

Are you wearing THAT hat? Are you playing THAT classical music? Is THAT body stretched and relaxed? Now you can go on to THIS next part. Be sure to color the duck.

The Silly Little Duck Story

Did you hear the one about the duck (*el pato*) who couldn't say the **ck** sound? Instead of "Quack, quack," he said "Qual, qual"! Well, *el pato* (the duck) went on vacation to Mazatlán and needed to buy *un sombrero* (a hat) because it was so hot and sunny. So he went to the first *mercado* (market) he could find. The salesman had *sombreros* of every shape and color and kept recommending different hats to the little *pato,* who kept repeating "¿Qual, qual?" And then the salesman would bring out another hat and would ask, "¿Este sombrero? ¿Ese sombrero?" The little *pato* kept quacking, "Qual."

After about fifteen minutes of this madness, the salesman finally plopped the biggest and most colorful *sombrero* he had on the head of the little *pato* and the duck exclaimed, "*¡Éste!*" which means "**This one!**" At that moment it dawned on the little duck that all the time he'd been quacking "Qual," he was actually asking: "Which one?"; so of course the salesman would say, "*¿Este sombrero?*" (this hat?) or "*¿Ese sombrero?*" (that hat?)

The duck and the salesman were so happy to have cleared up the confusion that they went to *la cantina* (the bar) for *una bebida* (a drink). Well, they ordered *"Dos bebidas, por favor"* (two drinks, please), but the waiter brought a whole tray of *bebidas* and began to ask, "*¿Esta bebida? ¿Esa bebida?*" and the duck would quack

38

"Qual" (which is actually spelled *Cuál* in Spanish) and the *sombrero* salesman, who had been through enough of **that** already, just picked out two big, cold *limonadas* and said decisively: "¡**Éstas!** *Una para tí, una para mí*"* which means "one for you, one for me." And that was that!

*Pronounced like **pot o' tea** and **pot o' me**

THIS = este, esta   THAT = ese, esa   THESE = estos, estas   THOSE = esos, esas

Are you scratching your head and wondering why *this* chapter is called "Hugging and Kissing"? Because you just learned about the *demonstratives,* and a demonstrative person is someone who shows affection by hugging and kissing! ***This** (este, esta),* **these** *(estos, estas),* **that** *(ese, esa),* **those** *(esos, esas)* are called *demonstrative adjectives.*

Remember that demonstrative adjectives always go hand in hand with (or agree with) a noun, so *este/ese* are masculine singular and go with a masculine singular noun. *Esta/esa* are feminine singular and go with a feminine singular noun. *Estos/esos* are masculine plural and go with masculine plural nouns. *Estas/esas* are feminine plural and go with feminine plural nouns.

Here's a way to tell the difference between *este,* "this here"; or *ese,* "that there." There's a *t* in *este, esta, estos, estas* (this, these). Think of the *t* as an arrow pointing to "this here."

this hat	this drink	these hats	these drinks
esTe sombrero	esTa bebida	esTos sombreros	esTas bebidas

Just remember this rule: if you **hear** a *t,* it's over **here**!

Game: Let's Hug and Kiss

Below is a list of nouns. Next to each one, depending on whether the noun is singular or plural, write in the demonstrative adjective in English: *this* or *that* / *these* or *those.* There is no right answer, just pick anything!

_____ man   _____ packs of gum

_____ boy   _____ bicycles

_____ girl   _____ baby boy

_____ children   _____ teenage girl

_____ cows   _____ businessman

Here are some Spanish words. They are all singular but may be either masculine or feminine. Write the demonstrative adjective *este* or *esta,* which, as you know, means "this."

_____ casa   _____ calculadora

_____ triciclo   _____ computadora

_____ libro   _____ cabeza

_____ mesa   _____ hombro

_____ hoja   _____ pierna

Now make the nouns plural by adding an *s* to each of the same words below. You will have to change the demonstrative adjective to *estos* or *estas.* For example: *estas casas.*

_____ casa___   _____ calculadora___

_____ triciclo___   _____ computadora___

_____ libro___   _____ cabeza___

_____ mesa___   _____ hombro___

_____ hoja___   _____ pierna___

→ *Answers and word meanings are at the end of the chapter.*

What's a Kel?

A kel is a different way than *ese* to say "that" in Spanish. It means "that over there, farther away from you than *ese.*" It's really spelled *aquel,* not *a kel,* in the masculine singular form. The feminine form is *aquella.* The plural forms are *aquellos* and *aquellas.* These last three sound like this: *a-**kay**-ya, a-**kay**-yos, a-**kay**-yas.* Say these out loud a couple of times just for fun.

If you want to practice using *that* in Spanish, here is the list of nouns again. Write in the singular demonstrative adjectives **ese, esa,** or **aquel, aquella.** Remember *ese* means "there," not "here," and *aquel* means "over there, farther away." And don't forget that ***-o*** words are masculine, ***-a*** words are feminine.

_____ casa   _____ calculadora

_____ triciclo   _____ computadora

_____ libro   _____ cabeza

_____ mesa   _____ hombro

_____ hoja   _____ pierna

➡ *Answers at the end of the chapter.*

Lonely Demonstratives

If you leave a demonstrative all alone, just *este* and *esta,* it means "this one"; and if you say the plural ones all alone, *estos* and *estas,* they mean "these ones." *Ese* and *esa* mean "that one" and *esos, esas* mean "those ones." They are called *demonstrative pronouns,* because pronouns go in place of a noun. Instead of "this hat," you are saying "this one."

How, you may be asking, can you see the difference between demonstrative adjectives and pronouns in Spanish, if they are all spelled the same? Easy! You put an accent mark or squashed bug on the **pronouns**, like this: *éste, ésta, éstos, éstas, ése, ésa, ésos, ésas.*

In the space below draw a round mouth with some big lips and two long arms. Then, write in what you have learned in this chapter on hugging and kissing.

Have you been reviewing the Lulu, Lola, Lalo and the Yoyo games? Do you spring out of bed every morning and cry **Parangaricutirimicuaro***?*

Don't forget to draw a picture, perhaps a little duck, next to Chapter 4 in the Contents!

Answers to "Let's Hug and Kiss" (Spanish version)

esta casa	esta calculadora
este triciclo	esta computadora
este libro	esta cabeza
esta mesa	este hombro
esta hoja	esta pierna

estas casas	estas calculadoras
estos triciclos	estas computadoras
estos libros	estas cabezas
estas mesas	estos hombros
estas hojas	estas piernas

esas (aquellas) casas	aquellas (esas) calculadoras
esos (aquellos) triciclos	esas (aquellas) computadoras
aquellos (esos) libros	aquellas (esas) cabezas
esas (aquellas) mesas	esos (aquellos) hombros
aquellas (esas) hojas	aquellas (esas) piernas

Word meanings: house, calculator, tricycle, computer, book, head, table, shoulder, leaf, leg

Answers to "Review" on page 43

1. **ee**-lo **oh**-ha **na**-tha os-pee-**tahl** **ya**-vay **ee**-so **yay**-gah oo-nee-vair-see-**thath** **pee**-nyah eem-por-**tahn**-tay
2. Masculine: pavo, palo, mono, payaso, pato
   Feminine: amiga, palapa, paleta, tina, hoja
3. tree tall, hats greens, houses bigs, grandmothers olds
4. KAY/K
5. Como
6. QUAL (Cuál)
7. My, your, his, her, your, their
8. The cat fat climbed the tree tall and ate the bird red.

REVIEW

Here is a short, easy quiz (answers are on the preceding page).

1. How do you pronounce: hilo   hoja   nada   hospital   llave   hizo   llega
   universidad   piña   importante?

2. Are these words masculine or feminine?

   pavo ___   amiga ___   palapa ___   palo ___   paleta ___   tina ___

   hoja ___   mono ___   sombrero ___   payaso ___

3. Cross out the incorrect words and write them correctly as if they were in
   Spanish:

   tall tree   _____

   blouse blue   _____

   hats green   _____

   big houses   _____

   old grandmothers   _____

4. How do you pronounce *que* in Spanish? _____

5. What lake in Italy means "how" or "what" in Spanish? _____

6. What did the little duck say, meaning "which" in Spanish? _____

7. What does "Me too, Sue"—*mi, tu, su*—mean in Spanish? _____

8. How would you say "The fat cat climbed the tall tree and ate the red bird"
   if you translated it word for word from Spanish?

   _____

Take a BIG break!

Congratulations!   In Spanish: **¡Felicitaciones!**

5

Who's Who?

CINCO

Before you begin, close your eyes, and think of a special, wonderful vacation that you have taken. Where did you go? What did you do? Who went with you? What was the best part of all? You can play soft music or just picture the memories. It's important when you prepare to learn something new, to prepare your brain with an exercise like this one. Now you are ready to go on.

What's missing in this picture? People! Persons! (*Personas*, in Spanish.)

I, you, he, she, it, we, you, they are called *personal* or *subject pronouns*. They're called subject pronouns because you'd get tired of saying Pablo did this and Pablo did that, and Pablo did something else, and Pablo didn't do that. Instead, you can just say "he." A **pro**noun fills in when you're just plain tired of using the noun. A subject pronoun is the person or thing doing the action, as in "I dance," or "He used to play soccer," or "It smells funny."

In Spanish there are five singular **pro**nouns (referring to just one *persona*) and five plural **pro**nouns (referring to more than one *persona*). Total: ten personal **pro**nouns. One of them, however, is only used in Spain.

Your Turn to Draw!

Next to each personal pronoun below, draw a little stick figure of *you* pointing to each person. Use the space in the margin on the left.

I   The first person, the one who is speaking (look out for number one) or doing the action, as in "I play soccer." Draw yourself pointing to yourself.

You   The second person, the one to whom you are speaking. In Spanish there are two ways of addressing people. One is the familiar or intimate (your family, your friends, babies, pets); the other is formal (someone you respect, someone older or whom you don't know well). Draw a picture of yourself pointing to your best friend or spouse, your pet, or a baby.

He, she, it   The third person, the one you are speaking about. It could also be the tree or the vacuum cleaner, which in Spanish, as you know, has to be either masculine or feminine. There is no word for *it* in Spanish, because there is no such thing as a neuter noun! Draw a picture of yourself pointing to a boy or man, a girl or woman, a favorite pet, and an object like a chocolate bar or a rose.

We   The first-person plural. *We* refers to more than one person doing the action or speaking along with you. Draw a picture of yourself with your arm around someone else.

You all (y'all)   The second-person plural. That is, when you're talking to more than one person at the same time. In Spanish there is just one word for *y'all*, whether you're on intimate or formal terms with them. Draw a picture of yourself pointing to a group of people.

They (the guys, the girls, the objects)   The third-person plural, or the people or things we're gossiping or talking about. In Spanish that could be "they" the men, or "they" the women, or even "they" the men and women. Or "they" the apples or vacuum cleaners! Draw a picture of yourself pointing to groups of people, and also pointing to several pieces of fruit.

Did you do the drawings yet? If not, go back and do that now.

Personal or subject pronouns

Singular		Plural	
English	Spanish	Spanish	English
I	yo	nosotros	we
you	tú (*intimate, familiar*)	vosotros (*Spain only*)	you
he, it	él	ellos	they (*m.*)
she, it	ella	ellas	they (*f.*)
you	usted (*formal*)	ustedes	you all (*m., f.*)

He, She, It

You may be questioning why *él* and *ella,* which mean "he" and "she," are also used for the pronoun *it.* Remember how all nouns have to have a gender, that is, they are either masculine or feminine, even if they are inanimate objects? It follows that when you are using the pronoun *it* to replace a chocolate bar or a rose, that pronoun would also have to have a gender, masculine or feminine.

El or *Él*?

Note: when someone is speaking, the sound of *él* and *el* is the same. When written, just plain *el* is the masculine article, the opposite of *la.* The pronoun *él,* with an accent, means "he" or "it."

Ud. and *Uds.*

Here's a thorny issue that has plagued Spanish teachers the world over. The pronoun *usted* is used for the formal *you. You* is technically the second person, the person to whom you are speaking, but it is **not** placed in second place, along with *tú.* Instead, it goes in third place along with *he, she, it,* and is considered a third-person personal pronoun. It should be up in second place, along with *tú,* don't you think? After all, in English, *you* is always the second person.

Centuries ago, *usted* meant something like "your mercy" (*merced,* in Spanish, like the girl's name Mercedes) or "your grace," which was how you addressed the duke, the count, the queen, or the king, as you bowed or curtsied. It was so very formal (compared to *tú,* which was and is still used with someone you love or know well, with babies, pets, people your age, friends, etc.) that it was almost as though you were talking to a third person (he or she) because that person was so far removed from you, or the puny little first person *I.* So, that's why *usted* is placed in the third, not the second place. Remembering that *usted* is third person will be very important when you get to Chapter 6 and beyond.

By the way, you will often see *usted* abbreviated in Spanish books like this: *Ud.* And the plural, *ustedes,* looks like this: *Uds.* But that is strictly when it's written. You always will sound out the full word, *usted* or *ustedes,* when addressing someone. Like this: oos-**teth** and oos-**te**-thays. (Make the *th* sound like the **th** in *they,* not in *teeth.*) Say *usted, ustedes* a couple of times out loud to get used to the sound.

A Regional Pronoun

In Argentina and Costa Rica there is a pronoun called *vos* that is used when you are talking to close, familiar friends. If you ever go there, you will hear it everywhere and learn to use it. No book will ever teach you this. It's sort of like a dialect.

Mixing Up the Sexes

You learned that *ellos* can mean "they" masculine or feminine. If you have a group of men or boys you're talking about, you say *ellos*. But if you have a group of men and women, or boys and girls you're talking about, you also say *ellos*. The male or masculine pronoun dominates in the Latin culture! Even if you have 1,000 females (*ellas*) in a big room, and one little baby boy, *él,* you have to say *ellos* when talking about them, which is masculine plural.

The Who Game

Write a personal pronoun underneath each of the figures below, **first in English, then in Spanish**. For example, under picture 1 you should write: **I/yo** because the person pictured is pointing to him- or herself.

◆ *The answers are at the end of the chapter.*

Now remember to go to the Contents and draw a symbol for the chapter. It will help you later on!

Answers to "The Who Game"

1. I/yo	4. they/ellos	7. informal you/tú
2. he/él	5. we/nosotros	8. they (*f.*)/ellas
3. she/ella	6. formal you/usted	9. you all/ustedes

Start out by doing a short relaxation exercise. Go to the beach in your mind. Then, drink a big glass of water to feed your brain. Next, "unroll" the edges of your right ear, then your left ear. This will help your right and your left brain work together! Finally, stand up and touch your left knee with your right hand, then, touch your right knee with your left hand. Do this several times. Now bring your right heel up behind you and touch it with your left hand, bring your left heel up behind you and touch it with your right hand. Do this several times. All of these things will help you learn more easily. Now, begin playing baroque or classical music.

Endings and Beginnings

'Burbs . . . verbs (remember about *b*s and *v*s?)

Verbs are actions that always go hand in hand with people, with personal or subject pronouns. I AM, you EAT, he RUNS, she SWIMS, we GO, you all WANT, they SING.

Infinitives

To be, to eat, to run, to swim are called *infinitive verbs.* The good news is there are only two things to remember about infinitive verbs in Spanish:

1. They are just one word, not two, as in English (to eat).

2. They always end in *-ar*, *-er*, or *-ir*.

Here is what infinitive verbs look like in English and Spanish. Say them aloud in Spanish and accent the *-ar*, *-er*, *-ir* ending each time:

English	Spanish
to communicate	comunic**ar**
to explore	explor**ar**
to dominate	domin**ar**
to admire	admir**ar**
to study	estudi**ar**
to comprehend or understand	comprend**er**
to sell	vend**er** (like a vendor)
to respond or answer	respond**er**
to insist	insist**ir**
to prefer	prefer**ir**
to decide	decid**ir**

Conjugating Verbs

(*Verbos* in Spanish sounds like **bear**-bohs.)

When you add different endings to the verb to indicate different persons doing the action, you are *conjugating* the verb. It sounds sort of mysterious and fun, doesn't it? Everyone does it! I do, you do, he or she does, we do, you all do, and they do too. All of us personal pronouns are involved in verb conjugation. Take the verb "to communicate." When you conjugate the verb, or say it with each of the subject or personal pronouns, it looks like this:

I communicate
you communicate
he, she, it communicates
we communicate
you all communicate
they communicate

Simple, don't you think? In Spanish you conjugate the same way. The only catch is, the endings of the verb *communicate,* or *comunicar,* are **different** for each person, or each of the personal pronouns you learned in Chapter 5. There are six different endings, whereas in English there are only two, *-e* and *-es*. If you don't believe it, look at the verb "to communicate" above. Think about other verbs, like *to go, to do, to run, to eat.* Just two endings!

You will be happy to know that in this book, we will only learn five endings in Spanish, because the second-person plural one, *vosotros,* which comes after *nosotros,* is only used in Spain, and is sort of outdated in today's Spanish classrooms.

How Now Brown Cow?

Yo—O

When the first person *I* (*yo*) is doing the action (communicating, admiring, insisting) you simply take away or chop off the *-ar, -er, -ir* ending and add the letter *o*. That's all there is to it! Very easy!

I communicate: *comunico* (accent the next-to-last syllable: co-mu-**ni**-co)
I admire: *admiro* (accent the next-to-last syllable: ad-**mi**-ro)
I comprehend, or understand: *comprendo* (com-**pren**-do)
I sell: *vendo* (**ven**-do)
I insist: *insisto* (in-**sis**-to)

Isn't that fantastic? You can conjugate just about any Spanish verb in the present tense, in the first person, by adding *-o* instead of the *-ar, -er, -ir* ending. In fact, in the entire Spanish language, all but four *yo* endings are *-o*. (You will learn them later on.) Regular verbs are totally dependable. You just apply this easy formula and get the right answer every time. Just sing: *Yo-o-o and a bottle of rum!*

The Domino Game

What is the *yo (I)* or first-person form of each of the verbs below? Cross out the *-ar* and add *-o*.

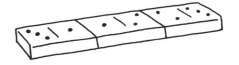

Group One Verbs (*-ar*)

dominar	admirar	solicitar
ocupar	depositar	plantar
investigar	optar	curar
observar	cultivar	calmar
ordenar	conspirar	visitar
pasar	comandar	invitar
marcar	transportar	necesitar
marchar	tolerar	inventar
concentrar	elevar	liberar
celebrar	explorar	pintar
colaborar	adoptar	causar
examinar	continuar	pronunciar
instalar	interpretar	calcular

Group Two Verbs (*-er*)

Now try these, using the same formula:

vender   comprender   responder

Group Three Verbs (*-ir*)

Finally, add the *-o* ending to these verbs:

    describir   insistir   decidir

➥ *Answers are at the end of the chapter.*

These verbs look very much like English, but if you're stumped as to what they mean, try adding *-ate* at the end, or simply remove the Spanish ending *(-ar, -er, -ir)*. Don't forget, when you are learning Spanish, that there are hundreds of cognate verbs, verbs that are similar to English, so it makes it very easy to understand them.

Check the Appendix for the meanings of the verbs in the three groups.

Verb Patterns

Now, look carefully at the following verbs from group one. Can you see a pattern?

domino — domina	ocupo — ocupa	solicito — solicita
paso — pasa	tolero — tolera	visito — visita

If you noticed that the new verb forms all ended in *-a*, you were right!

Now, look carefully at these verbs from groups two and three. Can you see a different pattern?

vendo — vende	comprendo — comprende
respondo — responde	suspendo — suspende
describo — describe	insisto — insiste
decido — decide	permito — permite

If you noticed that the new verb forms all ended in *-e*, you were right again!

In each pair, the verbs are in the first-person singular and the third-person singular.

The first-person singular, as you know, is *yo* (I). So, when you want to say "I observe," you say *observo*. No need to use *yo*, because the ending *-o* tells you automatically it's first person. When you want to say "I respond" (or "answer"), you say *respondo*. Easy! And when you want to say "I insist," what would you say? *Insisto*? Yes!

The third-person singular pronoun, as you know, is *él, ella* (he, she, it). When you want to say "he, she, it observes," you say *observa*. And when you want to say "he, she, it responds," you say *responde*. And for "he, she, it insists," you say *insiste*.

We actually skipped the second person and went right to the third-person singular. This way, learning the second-person singular later on will be much easier!

What About *Usted*?

Since *usted* is conjugated with *él* and *ella,* in the third person, the endings will be -*a* or -*e* just like the third-person singular verbs. So you also say *observa* and *responde* and *insiste* for the *usted* (formal you) form.

Can you make up a rule about -*ar* verb endings for the third-person singular? Write it below.

_____

_____

Can you make up a rule about -*er* and -*ir* verb endings for the third-person singular? Write it below.

_____

_____

➡ *Answers are at the end of the chapter.*

Advanced Dominoes

Write the *él, ella, usted* (third-person) form of each verb below. Since all the verbs are -*ar* verbs, this will be very, very easy.

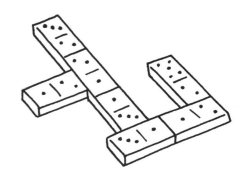

dominar	_____	transportar	_____
ocupar	_____	tolerar	_____
investigar	_____	elevar	_____
observar	_____	explorar	_____
ordenar	_____	adoptar	_____
pasar	_____	continuar	_____
marcar	_____	solicitar	_____
marchar	_____	plantar	_____
concentrar	_____	curar	_____

celebrar	_____	instalar	_____
colaborar	_____	visitar	_____
examinar	_____	invitar	_____
admirar	_____	necesitar	_____
depositar	_____	inventar	_____
optar	_____	liberar	_____
cultivar	_____	pintar	_____
conspirar	_____	causar	_____
comandar	_____	pronunciar	_____

Can you also do these verbs? They are *-er* and *-ir* verbs.

vender	_____	dividir	_____
comprender	_____	insistir	_____
responder	_____	decidir	_____

➧ *Answers are at the end of the chapter.*

-O/-A Tic Tac Toe Game

Here are some tic tac toe boards. Play against yourself using the *-ar* verbs in this chapter. Using the first-person singular *-o* as one player, fill in one space with a verb ending in *-o* for the first person. Then pretend you are the second player, and fill in another blank with a verb ending in *-a* for the third person. Now it's your turn again; fill in a space with another *-o* ending verb, and the second player uses a different *-a* ending. See who gets three in a row first! Like this:

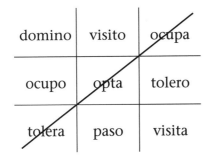
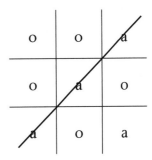

You can use any verb from the *-ar* list in the Domino game.

-O/-E Tic Tac Toe Game

Now play with -er and -ir verbs such as *describir, insistir, decidir, permitir, vender, comprender, responder,* and *suspender.*

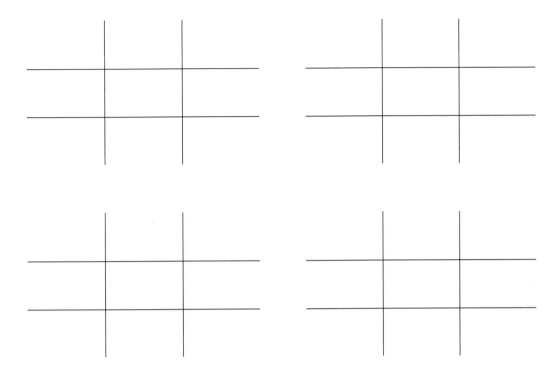

Did you beat yourself at tic tac toe?

Tenses and Moods

Incidentally, all these endings are for the *present tense*. A verb tense tells you when a verb is happening, or the time the action is happening, usually in the present, past, or future. **I go**, in English, is the present tense. **I went** is the past tense. **I will go** is the future tense.

The present tense is what is happening now. The verbs in this chapter are in the *present indicative*, because the present is in the *indicative mood*. *Indicative* means the verbs are positive; they are definite events, facts, or actions. And so far, all the verbs we've looked at in Spanish have been *regular verbs,* which means that they follow the same pattern when they are conjugated.

More Patterns

Now we are going to carry the patterns a teeny bit further. So far, you have learned these patterns for present tense verbs:

	-ar	-er	-ir
yo	-o	-o	-o
él, ella, usted	-a	-e	-e

If you just add an -s to the third-person endings above (-a, -e), you will have the second-person singular or *tú* form for each verb, -as and -es. If you want, go back and say each verb in Advanced Dominoes with an -s at the end, like this:

dominar	dominas	transportar	transportas
(Your turn!)			
ocupar	_____	tolerar	_____
investigar	_____	elevar	_____
observar	_____	explorar	_____
ordenar	_____	adoptar	_____
pasar	_____	continuar	_____
marcar	_____	solicitar	_____
marchar	_____	plantar	_____
concentrar	_____	curar	_____
celebrar	_____	instalar	_____
colaborar	_____	visitar	_____
examinar	_____	invitar	_____
admirar	_____	necesitar	_____
depositar	_____	inventar	_____
optar	_____	liberar	_____

cultivar	_____	pintar	_____
conspirar	_____	causar	_____
comandar	_____	pronunciar	_____

Can you also do these verbs? They are *-er, -ir* verbs.

vender	_____	dividir	_____
comprender	_____	insistir	_____
responder	_____	decidir	_____

So now the first-, second-, and third-person singular endings for verbs in the present tense look like this:

	-ar	-er	-ir
yo	-o	-o	-o
tú	-as	-es	-es
él, ella, usted	-a	-e	-e

Don't Put the Emphasis on the Wrong Syllable!

The most important thing to remember about verbs is their endings, and the second most important is the way to stress them when you speak. Most of us want to put the emphasis on the last syllable and say do-mi-**no**, do-mi-**nas**, do-mi-**na**. **No, no, no!** It should sound like this:

do-**mi**-no (do-**mee**-no), do-**mi**-nas, do-**mi**-na
ob-**ser**-vo, ob-**ser**-vas, ob-**ser**-va
com-**pren**-do, com-**pren**-des, com-**pren**-de
in-**sis**-to, in-**sis**-tes, in-**sis**-te

Put the accent on the next-to-last syllable. If you're starting a class, your teacher will insist on the correct pronunciation, so get a quick-start now and say them perfectly! Everyone in the class will be super impressed.

Army Version Dominoes

For this version you will take verbs from the first Domino game and **shout** or **sing** the first three persons, putting the emphasis on the next-to-last syllable.

1. Take your highlighter, and highlight the next-to-last syllable in each verb.
2. Pretend you are an army sergeant snapping at the platoon: Domino! Dominas! Domina!

If you can sing an army tune, like soldiers sing when they are marching, do that too! Otherwise, just yell loudly.

dominar	celebrar	transportar	instalar
ocupar	colaborar	tolerar	visitar
investigar	examinar	elevar	invitar
observar	admirar	explorar	necesitar
ordenar	depositar	adoptar	inventar
pasar	optar	continuar	liberar
marcar	cultivar	solicitar	pintar
marchar	conspirar	plantar	causar
concentrar	comandar	curar	pronunciar

The Last Two Endings

If you are really curious about the two remaining endings (the plural ones for *we* and *they/you all*), they are *-amos, -an* for *-ar* verbs; *-emos, -en* for *-er* verbs; and *-imos, -en* for *-ir* verbs. So, when you conjugate a verb in the present tense in its entirety it looks like this:

dominar	**comprender**	**insistir**
domino	comprendo	insisto
dominas	comprendes	insistes
domina	comprende	insiste
dominamos	comprendemos	insistimos
dominan	comprenden	insisten

Virgin Verbs

"Virgin verbs" are unconjugated verbs, left intact, with their *-ar, -er,* and *-ir* endings still attached. When do you leave a verb in its virgin, unconjugated form? When there are two verbs in the same sentence and the first one has already been conjugated—for example, after the verb "to need," *necesitar.* "I need to sell"—*Necesito vender.* Also, after expressions such as "it's possible," "it's impossible," and "it's important," you need not conjugate the verb that follows because the first one, "is," has been conjugated. (You will learn in Chapter 8 that the way to say "it is" in Spanish is *es.*) "It's important to concentrate."—*Es importante concentrar.* And "It's impossible to understand."—*Es imposible comprender.* Note that the formal term for virgin verbs is *infinitives.*

Summary

To conjugate Spanish verbs in most tenses—present, past, and future (*I paint, I painted, I will paint*)—you have to chop off the ending and get rid of it completely, then add a different ending for each personal pronoun. There are five endings, each one different and very recognizable. In fact, as you can tell from the ending which person is doing the action, you don't even need to use a personal pronoun if you don't want to.

Person	Ending	Example		
		-ar	-er	-ir
yo (I)	**o**	comunico	vendo	insisto
tú (you)	**as, es**	comunicas	vendes	insistes
él, ella, usted (he, she, you)	**a, e**	comunica	vende	insiste
nosotros (we)	**amos, emos, imos**	comunicamos	vendemos	insistimos
ellos, ellas, ustedes (they, you all)	**an, en**	comunican	venden	insisten

You will study these verb endings in your beginning level Spanish class, so knowing them now will definitely give you the quick-start you are looking for.

Mix and Match

Here is a practice game to make sure you can conjugate regular present tense verbs. Draw a line from the verb to the correct person. You can use the same personal pronoun more than once!

vendes	yo	comunicamos
observo	tú	usan
observas	él	vende
usamos	ella	domina
comunico	usted	observamos
comunican	nosotros	vendemos
domino	ellos	vendo
observa	ellas	usas
dominamos	ustedes	comunica

❧ *Answers are at the end of the chapter.*

If you're wondering whether or not to use the personal pronoun with the verb when speaking Spanish (as opposed to just conjugating the verb the way you have in the games in this chapter), the answer is yes!

Q & A Matching Game

Draw a line from each question in English on the left to the corresponding answer in Spanish on the right.

When someone asks you:	You answer in Spanish:
What do you do for a living?	Yo estudio los verbos.
Do you understand Spanish?	Yo celebro la Navidad (*Christmas*).
What are you all doing in the garden?	Yo deposito cheques.
Why are you reading *Quick-Start Spanish*?	Yo comprendo.
Why are you giving me a gift?	Yo vendo chocolates.
Why are you at the bank today?	Nosotros plantamos rosas.

➡ *Look at the end of the chapter for the answers.*

Boomerang Verbs!

Some verbs in Spanish are called *reflexive* verbs. This just means that, like a boomerang, the action comes back to the person doing the action. How is that possible? By doing the action to yourself: you can wash yourself, dress yourself, shave yourself, look at yourself in the mirror, put a hat on yourself, or call yourself (by your name). Let's consider them boomerang verbs, even though reflexive verbs is their official name.

If you wash the cat, dress the baby, shave the dog, look at a monkey, put a hat on a snowman, or call the doctor, these are non-boomerang verbs, that is, they are not reflexive verbs.

There are many other reflexive verbs in Spanish such as *to get married, to get fat, to become rich, to have fun, to fall in love.* Can you see how the action ultimately returns to you with these verbs?

When people meet each other, see each other, love each other, like each other, hug each other, kiss each other, marry each other, divorce each other, the actions require reflexive, or boomerang, verbs too. It takes two to tango when using these verbs, so you need to have plural personal pronouns such as *we* or *they.* We love each other; they kiss each other.

Recognizing a Boomerang or Reflexive Verb

In Spanish, a reflexive verb in the infinitive can be recognized by the way it ends: *-se. Lavarse* = "to wash oneself" (think of the word lavatory); *llamarse* = "to call oneself"; *enamorarse* = "to fall in love"; *divorciarse* = "to get divorced." Any time you see an infinitive verb that ends in *-se,* you know it's a reflexive verb.

Reflexive Verb Conjugation

You are probably wondering how to conjugate a reflexive verb. Remember *me llamo,* "my name is" ("I call myself") from "Before You Start"? *Llamo* is the first-person singular of an *-ar* verb with an *-o* ending. *Me* is a *reflexive pronoun.* There is a reflexive pronoun in Spanish for each personal or subject pronoun. The reflexive pronouns are:

me (goes with *yo*)
te (goes with *tú*)
se (goes with *él, ella, usted*)
nos (goes with *nosotros*)
se (goes with *ellos, ellas, ustedes,* just like in the singular!)

These reflexive pronouns are usually placed before the verb, like this:

llamarse (to call oneself)

me llamo (I call myself)
te llamas (you call yourself)
se llama (he, she, it, you call[s] himself, herself, itself, yourself)
nos llamamos (we call ourselves)
se llaman (they, you all call themselves, yourselves)

Since calling ourselves isn't really something we English-speakers do very often, let's conjugate another verb, *lavarse.* After all, we do wash ourselves every day! Some of the verbs are missing certain words, so you will have to fill them in.

lavarse (to wash oneself)

me lavo (I wash myself)

_____ lavas (you wash yourself)

se _____ (he, she, it, you wash[es] himself, herself, itself, yourself)

_____ lavamos (we wash ourselves)

_____ lavan (they, you all wash themselves, yourselves)

You can just copy or adapt from the verb before, if you get stumped.

Get Me to the Church on Time!

Here is a story using verbs which, if in Spanish, would all be boomerang or reflexive verbs. Please underline or highlight all the verbs starting with Mario's day.

Mario wakes up at 7:30. He gets up, washes his face, brushes his teeth, showers, washes his hair, dries himself, shaves, combs his hair, then gets dressed. He eats breakfast, puts on a top hat and dress coat, and goes off in his little sports car.

María wakes up at 8:00. She gets up, takes a shower, dries herself, brushes her teeth, styles her hair, puts on her makeup, puts on a beautiful gown, eats breakfast, and goes off in a black limousine.

Mario and María meet at the church. They kiss each other because they love each other so very much. That very day, they marry each other!

➧ *See the answers at the end of the chapter.*

 Draw a large boomerang. Inside it, write what you learned about boomerang verbs and about verb endings in general, from this chapter. It is the longest chapter in this book, so you may have to leaf back, look at the bold headings, and review what you learned. Your notes are for you alone, so there is no right answer! Don't forget to draw a picture in the Contents.

WHEW! YOU HAVE FINISHED THE LONGEST CHAPTER
IN THE BOOK. TAKE A BIG BREAK!

Answers to "The Domino Game"

Stress the syllable in **boldface.**

do**mi**no	ad**mi**ro	soli**ci**to
o**cu**po	depo**si**to	**plan**to
inves**ti**go	**op**to	**cu**ro
ob**ser**vo	cul**ti**vo	**cal**mo
or**de**no	cons**pi**ro	vi**si**to
paso	co**man**do	in**vi**to
marco	trans**por**to	nece**si**to
marcho	to**le**ro	in**ven**to
con**cen**tro	e**le**vo	li**be**ro
ce**le**bro	ex**plo**ro	**pin**to
cola**bo**ro	a**dop**to	**cau**so
exa**mi**no	con**ti**núo	pro**nun**cio
ins**ta**lo	inter**pre**to	cal**cu**lo
vendo	com**pren**do	res**pon**do
des**cri**bo	in**sis**to	de**ci**do

Answer for "What About *Usted*?"

-Ar verbs have *-a* endings, and *-er* and *-ir* verbs have *-e* endings for the third-person singular.

Answers to "Advanced Dominoes"

domina	transporta	celebra	instala
ocupa	tolera	colabora	visita
investiga	eleva	examina	invita
observa	explora	admira	necesita
ordena	adopta	deposita	inventa
pasa	continúa	opta	libera
marca	solicita	cultiva	pinta
marcha	planta	conspira	causa
concentra	cura	comanda	pronuncia

vende	comprende	responde
divide	insiste	decide

Answers to "Mix and Match"

tú vendes, yo observo, tú observas, nosotros usamos, yo comunico, ellos comunican, yo domino, usted (ella, él) observa, nosotros dominamos, nosotros comunicamos, ustedes (ellos) usan, ella (usted, él) vende, ella (usted, él) domina, nosotros observamos, nosotros vendemos, yo vendo, tú usas, ella (usted, él) comunica

Answers to the "Q & A Matching Game"

What do you do for a living?	Yo vendo chocolates.
Do you understand Spanish?	Yo comprendo.
What are you all doing in the garden?	Nosotros plantamos rosas.
Why are you reading *Quick-Start Spanish*?	Yo estudio los verbos.
Why are you giving me a gift?	Yo celebro la Navidad (*Christmas*).
Why are you at the bank today?	Yo deposito cheques.

Answers to the Mario and María story

(he) wakes up, gets up, washes his face, brushes his teeth, showers, washes his hair, dries himself, shaves, combs his hair, gets dressed, eats breakfast, puts on, goes off

(she) wakes up, gets up, takes a shower, dries herself, brushes her teeth, styles her hair, puts on makeup, puts on, eats breakfast, goes off.

(they) meet, kiss each other, love each other, marry each other

¿What Did You Say?
¡I Didn't Say Nuthin'!

SIETE

Use the space below to draw several big RED question marks.

Use this space to draw some GREEN upside-down question marks.

Like this: ¿ ¿ ¿ ¿ ¿ ¿ ¿ ¿ ¿ ¿ ¿ ¿ ¿ ¿ ¿ ¿ ¿ ¿

Questions

First we are going to talk about questions. There are two types of questions: yes or no questions and questions that start with question words such as *who, where, why, what, when, how, which,* etc.

Write some yes or no questions in the space below; for example, "Is the ocean blue?"

1. _____

2. _____

3. _____

4. _____

5. _____

When you want to ask a yes or no question in Spanish, it is so much easier than in English, where your questions have to start with *do, did, are, is, were*. In Spanish you just jump right in and say the verb and make your voice go up at the end, like a question.

¿Comunicas? = you communicate?
¿Venden? = they/you all sell?

Or, you can say the subject with the verb: *¿Tú comunicas? ¿Ustedes venden?*

When you write a question in Spanish, you must put an upside-down question mark before the question word! And a right-side-up one after the question!

Interview

Pretend you are interviewing someone to be your housemate or roommate.

Write five questions in English, and put an upside-down question mark before the question and a right-side-up one after it. Any question will do!

For example: ¿Do you sing in the shower? ¿Where did you live before?

1. _____
2. _____
3. _____
4. _____
5. _____

Now, go back and cross out all the *do/did*s, in order to make the questions sound the way they would in Spanish. Read the questions out loud.

The potential roommate also has a pet monkey. Ask three questions about the monkey. For example: ¿Does he eat bananas?

1. _____
2. _____
3. _____

Police Interrogation

A suspect has just been arrested for a major murder. You are the detective interrogating the subject, trying to find out as much as you can. Crossing out all the *do/did* words, write five questions that you might ask.

For example: ¿Where ~~did~~ you go last night? ¿~~Do~~ you own a gun?

1. _____

2. _____

3. _____

4. _____

5. _____

As you may have figured out from the title of the last game, the word for the type of sentence we've been talking about up until now is *interrogative* sentences. A sentence that is interrogative asks a question. A sentence that does not ask a question, but just states a fact, is an *affirmative* or *declarative* sentence, such as "The ocean is blue."

Super Sleuth

Since we're in the questioning mood, and since you are like a detective, sleuth, or investigator looking for hidden codes or clues in this book, it would be important to know how to say the six question words also called *interrogatives*: *What, when, how, who, where,* and *why.*

Remember the lake in Italy mentioned in Section One, Como? That means "how," but is used for "what" when you didn't hear what someone said. Well, when you go to Mexico instead of *¿Cómo?* you might hear *¿Mande?* which sounds like a day of the week (Monday) and means literally "Send it?" as in "Send that by me one more time?" Just don't make the mistake an overweight friend of mine made when he wanted to ask "How much?" at a restaurant, and repeated *"Como mucho"* to the waiter. The waiter kept answering *"Sí, sí"* (yes, yes), and bringing more food. My friend didn't realize he was really saying "I eat a lot"! The verb *comer* means "to eat." *Mucho* means "much."

The Two Chinese Brothers

Once upon a time there were two Chinese brothers, the KWAN brothers. The first brother's name was KWAN TOE and the second brother's name was KWAN DOUGH. KWAN TOE was a penny pincher and kept his money in his sock, next to his big toe. KWAN DOUGH was a baker, but he was very impatient especially when it took so long for the bread dough to rise.

That's because in Spanish the first brother's name meant "How much?" and the second brother's name meant "When?" Actually, in Spanish they're written *¿cuánto?* and *¿cuándo?*—and note that you accent or emphasize the **cuan** sound. (So now you know what the overweight man should have said, right? KWAN TOE!)

Next to each boldface word below, draw a symbol or picture that will help you.

What? = **¿qué?** (sometimes *¿Cómo?* or, in Mexico, *¿mande?*)

How? = **¿cómo?**

How much? = **¿cuánto?**

When? = **¿cuándo?**

Which? = **¿cuál?** (Remember the little duck?)

That leaves *who, where,* and *why.* Look at the pictures of three best friends. Your brain will remember their names. (Reminder: Use your crayons to color wherever there's a picture.)

| Kyen | Donday | Porkay |

And to see their names written properly in Spanish:

Who? = **¿quién?**
Where? = **¿dónde?**
Why? = **¿por qué?**

Exclamations

¿Guess what? ¡Exclamation points are the same as question marks—upside down at the start, right way up at the end! Practice making BLUE upside-down exclamation points below.

¡ ¡ ¡ ¡ ¡ ¡ ¡

Now write some of your favorite exclamations in English with an upside-down one first and a right-side-up one after. Examples: ¡WOW! ¡Great!

Here are some fun and useful exclamations you can say in Spanish.

¡Caramba! = Wow! **¡Salud!** = God bless you!

¡Hola! = Hi! **¡Adiós!** = Good-bye!

¡Ay! = Ow! Oh! **¡Fantástico!** = Great!

Negatives: ¡No! ¡No! ¡No! ¡No! ¡No!

When you want to say something in the negative, such as "I don't eat, he doesn't communicate, she doesn't go, we don't sell," you just use the word **no**: "I no eat, he no communicates, she no goes, we no sell." Kind of fun, eh?

Write the negative form of the following verbs, as though they were in Spanish.

He eats.	He no eats.	We can.	_____
She runs.	_____	She sells.	_____
We read.	_____	You dress yourself.	_____
They walk.	_____		_____
I go.	_____	They study.	_____
I play.	_____	She draws.	_____
He writes.	_____	It comes.	_____
They drive.	_____	We look.	_____

➡ *Answers are at the end of the chapter.*

Double Negatives

Remember how your teacher or mom always corrected you when you said, "I didn't see nothing, I'm not going nowhere, I'm not riding with nobody"? Well, in Spanish you are **allowed** to say those things! You use the double negative with *not, nothing, nobody, never, none,* etc.

Write some double negatives here in English, where you can get away with it, because you are just practicing your Spanish!

Examples: He didn't buy me nothing. She doesn't go nowhere.

1. _____

2. _____

3. _____

4. _____

5. _____

6. _____

➡ *See possible answers at the end of the chapter.*

Negative Words

Many negative words in Spanish begin with the letter *n,* just as they do in English:

not: **no**
neither . . . nor: **ni . . . ni** (nee nee)
never: **nunca** (**noon**-cah)
nobody: **nadie** (**nah**-theeay)
nothing: **nada** (**nah**-thah)

Snap your fingers and wiggle your hips as you repeat each negative word:

not, neither . . . nor, never, nobody, nothing!
not, neither . . . nor, never, nobody, nothing!

Now in Spanish:

no, ni . . . ¡ni, nunca, nadie, nada!
no, ni . . . ¡ni, nunca, nadie, nada!

A Very Negative Game

Draw a line from each Spanish sentence (A–F) to the one below that says the same thing in English (1–6).

A. ¡No comprendo nada!

B. Ana nunca decide nada.

C. El vendedor de sombreros no vende nunca en Buenos Aires.

D. Nunca planto nada en mi patio.

E. ¡Shh! No me observa nadie.

F. No exploramos ni el desierto Sahara ni el Kalahari.

1. I never plant nothing on my patio.

2. Ana never decides nothing.

3. Shh! Nobody is not observing me.

4. I don't understand nothing!

5. The hat salesman doesn't never sell in Buenos Aires.

6. We don't explore neither the Sahara nor the Kalahari desert.

❧ *Answers are at the end of the chapter.*

 Remember to draw a picture in the Contents!

Answers to "¡No! ¡No! ¡No! ¡No! ¡No!"

He no eats.
She no runs.
We no read.
They no walk.
I no go.
I no play.
He no writes.
They no drive.

We no can.
She no sells.
You no dress yourself.
They no study.
She no draws.
It no comes.
We no look.

Possible "Double Negatives"

He doesn't have no money.
We don't know nobody here.
I don't never have time.
She doesn't do nothing.
Don't you have none?
He doesn't never answer.

Answers to "A Very Negative Game"

A 4, B 2, C 5, D 1, E 3, F 6

8

"To Be" or Not "To Be"

OCHO

A Tale of Two Kingdoms

Long ago, before you were ever born, there was a country in which two separate kingdoms existed. One of the kingdoms was ruled by a king named Soy, and the other was ruled by his queen who called herself Es-toy.

As anyone might guess by its name, the people of Soylandia grew soybeans because the land was rich and fertile. Many varieties of grains, vegetables, and beans were produced in the kingdom of King Soy. The inhabitants, who were called Soylandians, were healthy and strong. They were tall, good-looking, and well developed. Some were blond and blue eyed, others were dark haired and green eyed, and others were red haired and freckled. They were honest people. Most of the people of Soylandia were either farmers or vendors who sold their produce to people of other kingdoms. You could tell that they were Soylandians just by the way they looked.

The kingdom (or queendom) of Es-toy was totally different. Es-toylandia was located east of Soylandia. As anyone might guess by its name, the people there were dedicated to the production of toys. And unlike the stable people of Soylandia, they were nomads and were constantly traveling from one place to another. Sometimes they were here, sometimes they were somewhere else: they were constantly going to other kingdoms, even other continents, marketing their wonderful toys. Whenever anyone thought of the Es-toylandians, he or she knew that these people were not really a permanent sort of people. Their lifestyle, unlike that of the Soylandians, was always in a state of flux. Sometimes the Es-toylandians were very happy; other times they were depressed. They were always very busy, and consequently they were tired and stressed out. As might be guessed, they were sick a lot, which made everyone very sad. But a few days later, they would once again be happy.

One day the king and the queen decided that they would try to unite the two kingdoms. They got together in Es-toylandia for a weekend. "What would it **be** like," began Queen Es-toy, "if we could **be** in the same royal castle and sleep in the same royal bed every night?" King Soy, who was a very sensitive man, a dreamer, and a romantic, smiled lovingly at his wife and said, "It would **be** wonderful!" But the next morning, the queen had to **be** in Tengolandia for a big toy sale. Tengolandia was a very needy country. The people there were always too hot or too cold, too hungry or too thirsty, and they were always sleepy and in a hurry. They were also very old. That's why Queen Es-toy wanted to sell them toys, to see if that would make things better. After that trip she had to **be** somewhere else, since she was always on the go.

After hours of talking, King Soy and Queen Es-toy finally realized that even though they very much wanted things to **be** different, they would probably never be able to **be** together. Queen Es-toy was just not the kind of person who could ever settle down in one place and **be** happy there. King Soy was a more stable person. He hated to leave home. So they decided to stay in their own kingdoms, **be** their own kind of person, running their own kingdoms with their own people. And they did live happily ever after!

This story illustrates two, actually three, ways of saying "I am" in Spanish. One way, you might have guessed, is *soy,* and the other is *estoy.* A third way, used in certain meanings, is *tengo.* We will get back to this story later on.

Now, close your eyes, play relaxing music, and picture the story of the two kingdoms. Open your eyes and, in the space below, draw a picture story of Soylandia, Es-toylandia, and Tengolandia and their rulers and inhabitants.

If the dialogue that follows were in Spanish, you would be using a lot of different "to be" verbs, which is what you are learning about in this chapter.

Blind Date

Knock, knock.

MARÍA ¿Yes?

PABLO Hello, **I'm** Pablo, your blind date. **I'm** from San Diego. **I'm** Mexican.

MARÍA **I'm** Peruvian. ¿How **are you**?

PABLO ¡**I'm** fine! ¡Caramba! ¡**You are** really beautiful!

MARÍA ¡**You're** pretty cute yourself! ¿**Is** that your red Porsche that **is** out front?

PABLO No, ¡sorry! **I'm** a student.

MARÍA ¿So where **is** your car?

PABLO My bicycle **is** in the driveway. We could walk to the park that **is** three blocks away.

MARÍA **I'm** too tired to walk. **I'm** a waitress, and **I am** on my feet all day.

PABLO ¿**Are you** thirsty? I'd like a beer. ¿How old **are you**?

MARÍA **I'm** 21. I can drive. My car **is** in the garage. **It's** a brand new Camaro.

PABLO ¿What **are we** waiting for? ¿Where **are** the keys?

MARÍA **I'm** looking for them. ¡Ay! I hope **they're** not lost. Here **they are**.

PABLO ¡**I'm** ready! ¡Let's go!

Now, read these questions and write the answers in complete sentences:

Who is he? __He is Pablo._____

Where is he from? _____

How is Pablo? _____

What does María look like? _____

What are their professions? _____

Where is the park? _____

How is she feeling? _____

How old is she? _____

Where is her car? _____

In English, we use the verb *to be* (*I am, you are, he is, she is, we are, you all are, they are*) like a big umbrella that covers all sorts of information about us: who we are, how we are, what we look like, where we are, what we are doing, what we're feeling.

To Be: Two or Three Verbs in Spanish

In Spanish there are two main verbs to express *to be*: *ser* and *estar*. That's where *Soy* and *Estoy* come from. *Tengo* comes from *tener,* which actually means "to have," but sometimes it means the same as "to be" in English.

Ser

Who are you?

I am Pablo (or John, or Mary, or Mr. Jones, or the President).
I am a student (or a painter, or a doctor, or a hairdresser).
I am from San Diego (or Bolivia, or the United States).
I am Mexican (or French, or German, or Italian).

What do you look like?

You are beautiful (or good-looking, or thin, or tall, or short, or fat).

Ser (or *soy*) expresses your "essence," WHO you are, your name, profession, nationality, and what you look like. *Ser* tells about things that are permanent and stable, like the people of Soylandia.

Estar

How are you?

I'm fine.
I'm tired (busy, angry, happy, impressed, tired, sick).

Where are you or where is it?

I am at home.
He is in San Francisco.
They are in Europe.
It is on the house.
He's around the corner.
It's parked out front.
I'm in here.

What are you doing?

I'm running.
She's reading.
I'm looking for my keys.
We're waiting for the bus.

When a "to be" verb has an *-ing* verb after it, you use *estar*. (More about this in Chapter 16.)

Estar (or *estoy*) expresses (1) feelings, (2) temporary conditions that could change the next day or sooner, and (3) where something or someone is (in a location). (4) It can also be used with *-ing* words (*jumping, running,* etc.) that describe what someone is doing right now.

Tener

> **Are you** thirsty?
> **He's** sleepy.
> **I'm** in a hurry.
> **We're** freezing!

Tener literally means "to have," but is used in Spanish with being hungry, thirsty, cold, hot, in a hurry, sleepy, and to express age. You say *tengo* (sounds like the name of a dance they do in Argentina, the tango!) to mean "I have the sensation of being hot or hungry or cold"; or "I have lived for 12 years or 23 years or 39 years."

Now, draw **yourself** on this page, and say the permanent things about you: your name (your Spanish name—this is different from saying *me llamo,* "my name is"), what you look like, if you are tall, short, thin, blond; and what you are like: romantic, a dreamer, a realist, an optimist. Write where you come from, your nationality. Write *SOY* next to yourself in BIG LETTERS!

Now write **ESTOY** in BIG LETTERS at the top of the blank space below.
Draw six or eight faces underneath. Now make the faces sad, happy, sick, tired, angry, depressed, excited, frustrated, etc. This means "I am" sad or happy or tired or angry or depressed or excited or frustrated.

Write **ESTÁ** in BIG LETTERS in the blank space below. This means "he, she, or it is."

Now draw a house, a tree, and a street in a city. In your picture, put:

a sun in the sky
a bird in the tree
a car or bicycle in the street
a bank in the city
an airplane below the sun
a person in front of the house
a park in the middle of the town

Write *está* in small letters under the sun, the bird, the car or bicycle, the bank, the airplane, the person, and the park.

Write *TENGO* in BIG LETTERS in the blank space below. Now, draw the foods, drinks, snacks you'd have if you were hungry and thirsty now. What would you wear if you were hot or cold? Write your age in big letters. (Remember that in your new identity you can be any age you want!)

The Dating Game

Take a blue, a yellow, and a green highlighter, marker, or crayon. Below is the story of the first date of Pablo and María from earlier in this chapter.

In BLUE, highlight or underline every boldface verb that answers the question **who** (name, profession, where the person is from), or shows a permanent quality, such as beautiful or cute.

In YELLOW, highlight or underline every boldface verb that describes **how** someone is feeling (fine, happy, sad, tired, busy, sick), **where** something or someone is, or **what** someone is **doing**.

In GREEN, highlight or underline every boldface verb showing desires or **sensations** of being thirsty, cold, sleepy, etc., as well as **how old** someone is.

Knock, knock.

MARÍA ¿Yes?

PABLO Hello, **I'm** Pablo, your blind date. **I'm** from San Diego. **I'm** Mexican.

MARÍA **I'm** Peruvian. ¿How **are you**?

PABLO ¡**I'm** fine! ¡Caramba! ¡**You are** really beautiful!

MARÍA ¡**You're** pretty cute yourself! ¿**Is** that your red Porsche that **is** out front?

PABLO No, ¡sorry! **I'm** a student.

MARÍA ¿So where **is** your car?

PABLO My bicycle **is** in the driveway. We could walk to the park that **is** three blocks away.

MARÍA   **I'm** too tired to walk. **I'm** a waitress, and **I am** on my feet all day.

PABLO   ¿**Are you** thirsty? I'd like a beer. ¿How old **are you**?

MARÍA   **I'm** 21. I can drive. My car **is** in the garage. **It's** a brand new Camaro.

PABLO   ¿What **are we** waiting for? ¿Where **are** the keys?

MARÍA   **I'm** looking for them. ¡Ay! I hope **they're** not lost. Here **they are**.

PABLO   ¡**I'm** ready! ¡Let's go!

Finished? If so, you should have 10 blue verbs, 15 yellow verbs, and 3 green verbs. (See the answers at the end of the chapter.) Can you tell that *ser* verbs are blue, *estar* verbs are yellow, and *tener* verbs are green?

Review

Which "To Be" Am I?

Label the following pictures with one of the following verbs: ser, estar, tener.

➡ *Answers are at the end of the chapter.*

   Don't forget to draw a picture next to Chapter 8 in the Contents!

Answers to "The Dating Game"

Blue verbs, *ser*: I'm Pablo, I'm from, I'm Mexican, I'm Peruvian, You're beautiful, You're cute, Is that?, I'm a student, I'm a waitress, It's a Camaro
Yellow verbs, *estar*: How are you, I'm fine, is out front?, is your car?, bicycle is, park that is three blocks, I'm tired, I'm on my feet, car is in, are we waiting, where are, I'm looking, they're lost, they are, I'm ready
Green verbs, *tener*: are you thirsty, how old are you?, I'm 21

Answers to "Which 'To Be' Am I?"

Ser: thin man, astronaut, USA person
Estar: riding a bike, boy jumping, sick person, happy person
Tener: sleepy person, freezing cold person, boy is six years old

Boy, Oh Boy!

Once I saw a cartoon showing a middle-aged couple sitting at the travel agent's desk looking at travel brochures for exotic places. The husband was explaining, "We'd like to go somewhere without any irregular verbs."

Irregular verbs don't follow the rules or the pattern that regular verbs do.

Irregular verbs
don't follow
the rules.

You may wonder why it is that they have to go and complicate a perfectly logical language like Spanish with verbs that don't follow the rules. Take the verb *ir* (pronounced *ear*, except you roll the "r"), which looks a lot like someone forgot the root or stem and just left the ending dangling (remember *-ar, -er, -ir*?).

The Verb *Ir*

Ir is one of the most important verbs in the whole language because it means "to go." How can you ever get anywhere without it?

The way to say these five verb conjugations is fun and simple:

voy (boy)	I go, I am going
vas (bas)	you go, you are going
va (ba, as in "Bah humbug!")	he, she, it goes, he, she, it is going
vamos* (bamos)	we go, we are going
van (ban, sounds like "bonbon")	they go, they are going

*Vamos means "Let's go!"

Actually these forms are sort of catchy. Say them quickly as you snap your fingers. You are free to shake your shoulders if you want!

The Verb *Dar*

The verb *dar,* which means "to give," is easy to conjugate because it rhymes with *ir.* Write the English verb forms to the right of the Spanish ones.

doy	I
das	you
da	he, she, it, you (formal)
damos	we
dan	they, you all

The Verb *Estar*

You already know another important irregular verb. Remember one that means "to be," *estar?* Well, *estar* also rhymes with *ir* and *dar.*

estoy

estás

está

estamos

están

Note: the stress is the same as for *dar:* es**toy**, es**tás**, es**tá**, es**tamos**, es**tán**.

The Verb *Ser*

You're probably wondering about *ser,* the other "to be" verb, right? Well, it only rhymes in the first person, as you already know: *soy.* The rest goes like this:

soy

eres

es

somos

son

If you want, you can take the verb apart and analyze it so that it makes sense, and you can probably find a pattern. Otherwise, just say the verb snapping your fingers and it'll be easier! Or try jumping up and down while you say the forms.

Now you know the four verbs that don't end in -*o* in the present tense: *soy, voy, doy, estoy!*

The Verb *Tener*

Tener, pronounced "ten-**air**" ("to have"), is another irregular verb already mentioned in the previous chapter. The first person is *tengo,* as in Tengolandia, so I like to call it a *-go* verb, because the first person in *-go* verbs always ends in *-go.* There are several more like it.

Draw a circle around the center and draw a flower petal around each *-go* verb to form one big flower. Then, match each *-go* verb with its infinitive below. Print the infinitives inside the petals.

vengo   pongo

tengo   salgo

-go
verbs
oigo   hago

digo   traigo

caigo

poner / tener / traer / hacer / oír / caer / venir / salir / decir

◆ *See the end of the chapter to find out the answer and the meaning of these verbs.*

Stem-Changing Verbs

Tener also happens to be a **stem-changing** verb. What's a stem-changing verb? A verb in which one letter in the infinitive stem sometimes changes to different letters. With the verb *tener,* in the stem *ten* the letter *e* changes to *ie,* that is, *ten* changes to *tien.* Here's how it looks as you conjugate the verb:

I	tengo (doesn't follow the stem change)
you	tienes
he, she, it, you (formal)	tiene

Another *e* to *ie* verb is *preferir,* "to prefer." With this verb, the change also occurs in the first-person (I) form. Here's how it looks as you conjugate it:

prefiero
prefieres
prefiere

The other frequently used stem change is an *o* that changes to *ue*. One *o* to *ue* verb is *costar,* "to cost." When you change the stem, it becomes:

cuesto
cuestas
cuesta

BEWARE!
Stem-changing verbs:
e–ie, o–ue

Here are some stem-changing verbs that follow the models for *preferir* and *costar.* It doesn't matter if you know what they mean, although you may look at the end of the chapter if you are really interested. Write in the first and third persons. The other endings aren't important for now.

Remember the endings: an *-o* for the first person; and for the third person, an *-a* for *-ar* verbs and an *-e* for *-er* and *-ir* verbs.

Have fun filling in the blanks:

preferir	prefiero–prefiere	costar	cuesto–cuesta
pensar		contar	
cerrar		jugar*	
comenzar		acostar	
sentir		volver	
entender		poder	
despertar		morir	

*This is actually a *u* to *ue* stem-changing verb.

➧ *See the answers at the end of this chapter. If you are an eager beaver and want to see the entire conjugation of all the verbs in this part, look in the Appendix.*

There are other stem-change models, but we have covered the most important ones here.

Have you been regularly rewarding yourself for your progress? This last chapter deserves TWO treats! But don't forget your picture in the Contents!

Answers to "The Verb *Tener*"

vengo–venir (*to come*) pongo–poner (*to put*) digo–decir (*to say*)
tengo–tener (*to have*) salgo–salir (*to go out*) hago–hacer (*to make, do*)
oigo–oír (*to hear*) caigo–caer (*to fall*) traigo–traer (*to bring*)

Answers to "Stem-Changing Verbs"

prefiero–prefiere cuesto–cuesta
pienso–piensa cuento–cuenta
cierro–cierra juego–juega
comienzo–comienza acuesto–acuesta
siento–siente vuelvo–vuelve
entiendo–entiende puedo–puede
despierto–despierta muero–muere

Verb meanings:
to prefer to cost
to think to count, tell
to close to play
to commence, begin to lie down
to feel to return
to understand to be able to
to wake up to die

Really and Truly the Shortest and Easiest Chapter!

DIEZ

Begin by doing a relaxation exercise. Would you like to go to the beach? Use the relaxation suggested in Chapter 1.

This is really and truly going to be the shortest and easiest chapter so far in this book . . . honestly!

Adverbs

Can you find the three words that end in *-ly* in the sentence above this one? These are *adverbs*. Adverbs actually describe or give you more information about verbs, as well as adjectives or other adverbs. For example: He walked **slowly** across the street, glancing **carefully** in every direction. **Quickly** he jumped up on the opposite curb, looking **nervously** over his left shoulder.

Each of these adverbs definitely went with a verb. Thus, ad-verb. In Spanish, adverbs frequently end in *-mente*. In English they usually end in *-ly*.

Spanish adjective (f.)	Spanish adverb	English adverb
honesta	honesta**mente**	honestly
franca	franca**mente**	frankly
sincera	sincera**mente**	sincerely
rápida	rápida**mente**	rapidly
frecuente	frecuente**mente**	frequently
obvia	obvia**mente**	obviously
clara	clara**mente**	clearly
absoluta	absoluta**mente**	absolutely
perfecta	perfecta**mente**	perfectly

Now, can you make adverbs out of these three adjectives?

Spanish adjective	Spanish adverb	English adverb
oficial	oficialmente	officially
real	_____	_____
personal	_____	_____
normal	_____	_____

➤ *Answers are at the end of this chapter.*

Shall I Compare Thee to a Summer's Day?

Go back to the title of this chapter, and find the two words that end in *-est.* Obviously (adverbs seem to be springing up all over!) we were comparing this chapter to all the other ones in the book. *Shortest* and *easiest* are not adverbs, since they modify the word *chapter,* which is a noun. That makes them adjectives, right? If you don't remember, go back to Chapter 2, "Color Me Blue."

When you are making a comparison between things or people or animals (that is, nouns), you use *comparative* and *superlative adjectives.* Obviously comparatives compare things, and a superlative is superior to all the rest.

Adjective	Comparative	Superlative
short	shorter	shortest
easy	easier	easiest

In Spanish there is no equivalent to the English *-er* or *-est* ending. Everything is just "more" or "the most." The word *más* is used for both.

Easy, Easier, Easiest

Draw lines from the English to the Spanish words. The first one is done for you.

easy	more easy (easier)	the most easy (easiest)
intelligent	more intelligent	the most intelligent
small	more small (smaller)	the most small (smallest)
big	more big (bigger)	the most big (biggest)
fácil	más fácil	el más fácil
inteligente	más inteligente	el más inteligente
chica	más chica	la más chica
chico	más chico	el más chico
grande	más grande	el más grande

What if someone is less intelligent or the least intelligent in the class? Instead of *más* you use *menos*. In fact, knowing these two words will help you when someone asks, "How are you?" (*¿Cómo está?*) in Spanish, and you can answer, "More or less" (*Más o menos*).

Now draw lines from the English to the Spanish, as you did before:

easy	less easy	the least easy
intelligent	less intelligent	the least intelligent
fácil	menos fácil	el menos fácil
inteligente	menos inteligente	el menos inteligente

One Step Farther

If you are making a comparison of two people or objects and want to point out that one person is more intelligent than another one, or one language is easier or less easy than another, use *que* (pronounced KAY, remember) for the word *than*. Can you read and translate these statements?

Paco es más inteligente que Pedro.

_____

María es menos inteligente que Dolores.

_____

El español es más fácil que el japonés.

_____

Los carros en Madrid son más chicos que los carros en Chicago.

_____

➧ *Answers are at the end of the chapter.*

Tan . . . Como

Are you measuring or counting pages to see if this is really the shortest chapter? Chapter 2 is as short as this one and just as easy. That's another way to make a comparison, when two things are equal. It's also called the comparative. The way to say "as . . . as" in Spanish is *tan . . . como* (remember Como, a lake in Italy?). For example: *tan inteligente como, tan grande como, tan alto como, tan interesante como*. And there you have it!

The Bigger? Smaller? Game

Look at the pictures below and identify the comparisons being made, first in English, then in Spanish.

Here are some adjectives you can use:

inteligente, grande, alto (tall, as in altitude), *bajo* (short or low, as in Baja California, which is Lower California), *chico, interesante*

For example, in picture 1 you can see that one car is bigger than the other car. Write *más grande que* under the bigger car; you can write either *menos grande que* or *más chico que* under the smaller car.

➡ *The answers are at the end of this chapter.*

 Well done, you've completed this section—but don't forget to draw a picture in the Contents!

Answers to "Adverbs"

realmente	really
personalmente	personally
normalmente	normally

Answers to "One Step Farther"

Paco is more intelligent than Pedro.

María is less intelligent than Dolores.

Spanish is easier than Japanese.

The cars in Madrid are smaller than the cars in Chicago.

Answers to "The Bigger? Smaller? Game"

1. más grande que; menos grande que, más chico que
2. más alta que; menos alta que, más baja que (Remember to change *o* to *a* to agree with the noun in gender.)
3. más grandes que; menos grandes que, más chicos que (Remember to add the *s* because the elephants and mice are plural!)
4. menos inteligente que; más inteligente que
5. más grande que; más chico que; menos grande que; el más chico; el más grande
6. tan grande como

REVIEW

A Little Fun Quiz: Multiple-Choice Answers

Circle the correct letter (answer).

1. *-ar, -er, -ir* are

    a. noises people make when they clear their throats in Mexico.
    b. infinitive verb endings.
    c. the first three letters of the Mayan alphabet.

2. The first-person singular conjugation for the present indicative always ends in _____ in Spanish.

    a. *-o*
    b. *-m*
    c. *-a* or *-e*

3. Reflexive verbs are like

    a. dominoes.
    b. tic tac toe.
    c. boomerangs.

4. *Mande,* when heard in Mexico, is

    a. a day of the week.
    b. the way people ask "What?"
    c. a Mexican sauce made from chocolate and spices, used on chicken.

5. The two Chinese brothers' names, when spelled correctly in Spanish, are

    a. Qual, Quack.
    b. Porky, Dorky.
    c. Cuánto, Cuándo.

6. People from Soylandia were

    a. hungry, hot and cold, sleepy old people.
    b. busy, tired, stressed-out nomads.
    c. tall, good-looking, honest farmers.

7. People from Es-toylandia were

    a. hungry, hot and cold, sleepy old people.
    b. busy, tired, stressed-out nomads.
    c. tall, good-looking, honest farmers.

8. People from Tengolandia were

    a. hungry, hot and cold, sleepy old people.
    b. busy, tired, stressed-out nomads.
    c. tall, good-looking, honest farmers.

9. When you say *voy* in Spanish, it means

    a. you're looking for a boy.

    b. you have your bowels and vowels mixed up.

    c. "I go" or "I am going."

10. "Stem-changing" means

    a. that certain types of cut flowers must be clipped every day.

    b. verbs change from *e* to *ie* or *o* to *ue* in the present tense.

    c. stems of plants change colors when a chameleon is climbing them.

11. The word *normalmente* in Spanish is

    a. someone who has a normal mind.

    b. an adverb meaning "normally."

    c. the normal way to combine a verb with an adverb.

12. In English, comparative and superlative adjectives end in

    a. *-er* and *-est*.

    b. *-tive*.

    c. none of the above.

13. In Spanish, comparative adjectives

    a. end in *-amos*.

    b. start with *más* or with *menos*.

    c. are a lot like a summer's day.

Answers

1 b, 2 a, 3 c, 4 b, 5 c, 6 c, 7 b, 8 a, 9 c, 10 b, 11 b, 12 a, 13 b

¡Bravo! ¡Olé! ¡Felicitaciones!

You have just completed the two most important sections in this book. You are now prepared for any beginning level Spanish class. Take a big, big break.

The next section is intended for second semester or intermediate level Spanish. You may wait until you've reached that level, or if you're having fun, by all means continue!

Also, use Sections Two and Three as a resource guide in any Spanish class, even second semester, second year, or advanced levels.

BUILDING MUSCLES

Now that you have covered the bare bones, or the essentials, of the structure of the Spanish language—i.e., the terms that will help you before day one of your Spanish class—it's time to start the tougher stuff. When you read and do the exercises in Chapters 11 through 20, it will be like working out at the gym, because these are the more serious parts of the structure of Spanish. But don't worry! This workout will be just as easy and fun for you as the first ten chapters.

Oops! There Are Those Pesky OPs!

ONCE

John throws the ball to Jake; Jake passes the ball to Susan; Susan tosses the ball to Kate; Kate punts the ball to Bob; Bob rolls the ball to Steve; Steve hits the ball to Beth; Beth kicks the ball to Jake. . . . If this were a ball game, at this rate no one would ever score a point! Also, there are too many repetitions of the words *the ball*. Why not just say *it*?

John throws what? Jake passes what? Susan tosses what? Kate punts what? Bob rolls what? Steve hits what? Beth kicks what? The DIRECT OBJECT is whatever they throw, pass, toss, punt, roll, hit, or kick. It answers the question "Who?" or "What?" The ball is the *direct object*. The *direct object pronoun* is the word you use instead of repeating the direct object (the ball, in this case) over and over and over.

The ball or it = *direct object*.

Direct object pronouns can also be people:

> Joe hugs **me**.
> I love **you**.
> Mary sees Jane. Mary sees **her**.
> Mary kisses Bill. Mary kisses **him**.
> The dog finds **us**.
> Mom feeds **them**.

The direct object pronouns are: *me, you, her, him, it, us, them*.

Jennifer tells a secret to Jane, Jane tells it to Jacob, Jacob tells it to Jonathan . . . like that game of "telegraph"!

It = *direct object pronoun*. The "secret" is the *direct object*.

But what about "to Jane, to Jacob, to Jonathan"? They are the *indirect objects*. "To her" is the *indirect object pronoun*.

The indirect object pronouns are *(to) me, (to) you, (to) her, (to) him, (to) it, (to) us, (to) them*.

> Joe gives **me** a hug. (He gives a hug to me.)
> I give **you** $100. (I give $100 to you.)
> Mary tells **her** the secret. (Mary tells the secret to her.)
> Larry passes **him** the ball. (Larry passes the ball to him.)
> John tells **us** a story. (John tells a story to us.)
> We loan **them** our stereo. (We loan our stereo to them.)

If the direct object can be identified by answering the question "Who?" or "What?," the indirect object can be identified by answering the question "To whom?" or "To what?"

Spanish Object Pronouns

What about Spanish? Spanish also has direct and indirect object pronouns. Let's call them "OPs"!

Direct object pronouns, or DOPs, look like this in Spanish:

> **me** (me)   (pronounced **may**)
> **te** (you)   (pronounced **tay**)
> **lo**, **la*** (him, her, it)   (Just remember LOLA!)
> **nos** (us)
> **los**, **las*** (them, you all)

*Lo and *los* refer to masculine nouns; *la* and *las* refer to feminine nouns.

Indirect object pronouns, or IOPs, look like this in Spanish:

> **me** (to me)
> **te** (to you)
> **le** (to him, to her, to it) (pronounced **lay**)
> **nos** (to us)
> **les** (to them, to you all)

In case you didn't notice, DOPs and IOPs in Spanish are similar, but not identical. Even though me, te, and nos are the same, the third persons are different. DOPs are lo, la, los, las; IOPs are le, les.

Game: DOP or IOP?

Highlight all the direct object pronouns, and circle the indirect object pronouns.

Example: Mary tells it to (me).

> John punts it to him.
>
> Jerry loans it to them.
>
> Pablo passes them to us.
>
> Carmen gives it to her.
>
> Jim tosses them to me.
>
> María writes it to him.
>
> Mr. Díaz faxes them to us.

➥ *Answers are at the end of the chapter.*

Two OPs at a Time

When you have **two** object pronouns together, as in "He gives it to me," it's pretty simple in English, since you use the word *to* before the IOP. In Spanish you put both object pronouns next to each other: *me lo, te la, nos los,* etc.

Sometimes, when you are using an order or command such as "Give *it* to *me*!," you merge the two object pronouns into a single word: *melo, tela, noslos,* etc. Strange, eh? You will find out more about this unusual grammar rule in Chapter 18.

DOPs and IOPs: Where Do They Go?

Object pronouns almost always come **before** the verb. IOPs almost always come **before** the DOP. So you say "John to me it throws." "Larry to us it passes." "We to them it give." And so on.

Game: ¡Reverso!

Take the following sentences in English and write them the way you would in Spanish.

English	Spanish
Mary tells it to me.	Mary to me it tells.
John punts it to him.	_____
Jerry loans it to them.	_____
Pablo passes them to us.	_____
Carmen gives it to her.	_____
Jim tosses them to me.	_____
María writes it to him.	_____
Mr. Díaz faxes them to us.	_____

➡ *The answers are at the end of the chapter.*

I Like, You Like, We All Like Bananas

There is a verb you will surely learn in your first-year Spanish class, called *gustar*. It means "to like." Literally this verb means "to be pleasing to."

Gustar is conjugated a little like the boomerang verbs, so you might be fooled by some of the pronouns that come before the verb: *me, te,* and *nos.* These are actually IOPs, indirect object pronouns. The two most important forms to learn at a beginner level are *me gusta* and *me gustan.*

For example, "I like coffee" is *Me gusta el café.* Literally "To me is pleasing coffee." (You remember from Chapter 1 that in Spanish an article is almost always used before nouns.) In the plural, "I like bananas" is *Me gustan las bananas.* This is because the verb has to be in the plural since the subject, *bananas,* is plural.

How would you say these three sentences in Spanish?

I like chocolate. _____

I like roses. _____

I like Mexican hats. _____

➡ *Answers are at the end of the chapter.*

Keep up the good habits. Draw a picture next to Chapter 11 in the Contents!

Answers to "DOP or IOP?"

DOPs: Mary tells **it** to me.
John punts **it** to him.
Jerry loans **it** to them.
Pablo passes **them** to us.
Carmen gives **it** to her.
Jim tosses **them** to me.
María writes **it** to him.
Mr. Díaz faxes **them** to us.

IOPs: Mary tells it to (me).
John punts it to (him).
Jerry loans it to (them).
Pablo passes them to (us).
Carmen gives it to (her).
Jim tosses them to (me).
María writes it to (him).
Mr. Díaz faxes them to (us).

Answers to "¡Reverso!"

John to him it punts.
Jerry to them it loans.
Pablo to us them passes.
Carmen to her it gives.
Jim to me them tosses.
María to him it writes.
Mr. Díaz to us them faxes.

Answers to *gustar* sentences

Me gusta el chocolate.
Me gustan las rosas.
Me gustan los sombreros mexicanos.

12

Poor Pablo!

DOCE

Before you begin the story about Pablo, do some light stretches. Stand up and rotate your arms, making big circles forward, then the opposite way. Touch your left foot or knee with your right hand; touch your right foot or knee with your left hand.

Now sit down and rub your palms together, then place them over your eyes, keeping your eyes open and feeling the warmth. Now do eye exercises: keeping your head straight, look up, down, up, down, up, down. Now look to the right, left, right, left, right, left. Now look to the upper right and lower left three times, then to the upper left and lower right three times. There! You have just done brain calisthenics!

Past Tense Verbs

Yesterday Pablo got up at 7 A.M. He shaved, got dressed, ate breakfast, brushed his teeth, left the house, walked to the corner, tripped over his shoelace, and fell down. A car hit him. At 9 A.M. an ambulance came and took him to the hospital. Poor Pablo!

You can finish the story of the rest of Pablo's day.

.

How many verbs can you count in Pablo's story? Circle them. You should have found twelve: *got up, shaved, got dressed, ate, brushed, left, walked, tripped, fell, hit, came, took.*

Every verb was in the past tense, the *preterite*. The preterite is the no-nonsense tense in the past, as in "I came, I saw, I conquered." It happened, no kidding! It's over and done with, and that's all there is to it. If you had to plot the action on a time line, you could put an *x* on the time or day or month or year that it happened. The action is clearly finished. A verb in the preterite is a single action.

Illustrate the time line below with Pablo's story, putting each event in sequence. Mark each event with an *x* on the line, including the events that you've added.

got up
   x
_____

Carmen's Cookie Game

This game is more fun when it's played by two or three people. Each person should have a Spanish name, and one should be Carmen. The first person, Carmen, snaps her or his fingers and starts out by saying: "**Who stole** the cookies from the *(pause)* cookie jar?" The next person says: "**Carmen stole** the cookies from the *(pause)* cookie jar." The first person exclaims, "Who, me?" (Players are still snapping their fingers in rhythm.) The person who just accused Carmen says, "Yes, you!" Carmen says, "Wanna fight?" The previous person says, "No, you're right." Then the second or third person goes back to the beginning but this time changes verbs: "**Who ate** the cookies from the *(pause)* cookie jar?" and so on, each time accusing a different player. Third time around, "**Who baked** the cookies . . . " or "**Who broke** the cookies . . . " or "**Who touched.** . . . "

If you can't find anyone to play the game with you, that's OK. Just snap your fingers and play alone, using different voices. Make sure you use at least five verbs, and if you are alone, you can use any crazy verbs you want. Make sure they are in the past, or the preterite.

The Parrot Joke

Highlight all the verbs in this story. They are in the preterite. Keep in mind that preterite questions in English always begin with *did/didn't.*

A businessman traveled to South America and went to the market to find a gift for his wife. He bought her a huge talking parrot and shipped it to her. When he returned home, the first thing he asked his wife was "Did you receive the bird I sent you?" "Oh, yes, thank you, my love," she answered. "How did you like it?" he asked. "I loved it!" she exclaimed. "I cooked it for dinner last night!" The husband became very angry and cried out, "You ate that bird for dinner? That parrot cost me $1,000. It spoke eight languages!" "Well," retorted his wife, "if it knew eight languages, how come it didn't say anything?"

➥ *Answers are at the end of the chapter.*

Now, can you draw a time line below, and plot all the verbs in this story on it?

Preterites: The Squashed Bugs Specialists

Now that you know about preterites, you're probably wondering how to recognize a preterite verb form in Spanish. The key is in the squashed bugs, or accent marks. Here are the first-person (*yo*) and the third-person (*él, ella, usted*) conjugations of some familiar infinitives:

Infinitive	Preterite
dominar	dominé, dominó
usar	usé, usó
explorar	exploré, exploró
visitar	visité, visitó
pasar	pasé, pasó

Do you see a pattern? Can you make a rule? Just complete the sentences:

The first-person ending for *-ar* verbs in the preterite is _____.

The third-person ending for *-ar* verbs in the preterite is _____.

Now practice just saying: é . . . ó, é . . . ó, é . . . ó! Pound on the table or clap your hands and repeat it! Then say the preterite forms of the -ar verbs above.

Here are some more verbs:

Infinitive	Preterite
vender	vendí, vendió
comprender	comprendí, comprendió
insistir	insistí, insistió
dividir	dividí, dividió

Can you see a pattern for these verbs? Can you make a rule? Just complete the sentences:

The first-person ending for -er, -ir verbs in the preterite is _____.

The third-person ending for -er, -ir verbs in the preterite is _____.

Now practice them: í . . . ió, í . . . ió, í . . . ió! Pound on the table or clap your hands and repeat it! Then say the preterite forms of the -er and -ir verbs above.

PRETERITE
exploré, exploró!
comprendí, comprendió!

You are, of course, remembering that the pronunciation in English would sound like this: "Ay! Oh!" for the -ar verbs and "Ee! Yoh!" for the -er, -ir verbs, right?

The Missing Persons

If you are interested in the other persons for preterite verbs, here they are:

Tú: **-aste** (for -ar verbs); **-iste** (for -er, -ir verbs)
Nosotros: **-amos** (for -ar verbs); **-imos** (for -er, -ir verbs) *Same as the present!*
Ellos, ellas, ustedes: **-aron** (for -ar verbs); **-ieron** (for -er and -ir verbs)

Let's put it all together:

-ar	-er	-ir
explorar	**vender**	**decidir**
exploré	vendí	decidí
exploraste	vendiste	decidiste
exploró	vendió	decidió
exploramos	vendimos	decidimos
exploraron	vendieron	decidieron

Read the three verbs out loud and toss the kush ball as you say them loudly and emphatically.

News Headlines

Read and translate the following newspaper headlines in Spanish.

Actor norteamericano admite, "¡Yo *visité* Cuba!"

¡Mecánico *instaló* un motor falso en un carro Corvette!

El criminal *declaró*, "¡Soy inocente!"

¡Dos dentistas *inventaron* pasta dental invisible!

¡Astronauta ruso *exploró* el planeta Urano en 1988!

➡ *Answers are at the end of the chapter.*

Those Darn Irregulars

Are there irregular verbs in the preterite too? Yep! They are so much fun to learn. Look at the words below. That's all you get, a word and a memory aid. You'll have to beg your Spanish teacher to tell you the whole verb. Or, look in the Appendix.

vino (like wine)   **quise** (kissee)   **puse** (pussy)   **pude** (Poody)

supe (soupy)   **hice** (eassy!)   **fui** (phooey!)

tuve (tooveh is grooveh, and so is estooveh) **estuve**

Here are the infinitives to these verbs. Can you match them up? Next to each infinitive below, write what you think is the correct irregular preterite.

Hacer   _____

Ir, ser   _____

Saber   _____

Poner   _____

Venir   _____

Tener   _____

Estar   _____

Querer   _____

Poder   _____

➡ *You will find the correct answers at the end of the chapter.*

 You hardly need reminding about drawing a picture in the Contents!

Preterite verbs in "The Parrot Joke"

traveled, went, bought, shipped, returned, asked, did you receive, sent, answered, did you like, asked, loved, exclaimed, cooked, became, cried, ate, cost, spoke, retorted, knew, didn't say

Answers to "News Headlines"

North American actor admits, "I visited Cuba!"
Mechanic installed a fake motor in a Corvette car!
The criminal declared, "I'm innocent!"
Two dentists invented invisible toothpaste!
Russian astronaut explored the planet Uranus in 1988!

Answers to matching irregular preterites

Hacer	hice
Ir, ser	fui
Saber	supe
Poner	puse
Venir	vino
Tener	tuve
Estar	estuve
Querer	quise
Poder	pude

13

I Ain't Perfect, but I'm All I've Got!

TRECE

Before you begin this chapter, close your eyes and remember a pleasant or happy event that happened to you in the past. Recall all the details, sights, sounds, smells, and feelings of that event. Relive each second, as you feel yourself being there all over again. When you are finished, slowly open your eyes and stretch.

Nieve: A Story About Snow

Once upon a time there was a little boy named Carlos. Carlos lived in a *pueblo* (small town) in Mexico. He was five years old. Every day when he walked to *la escuela* (school), he listened to the birds that were singing in the trees. It was always very hot in his *pueblo. El sol* (sun) shone down on Carlos's head each day, so he always wore a big straw *sombrero* (hat). On his way to school, Carlos used to daydream about what snow was like. In school he would sit and look out the window, and he wished it would snow. He had never seen snow. But even though he waited and wished and hoped, it never snowed.

Every year on Christmas Eve, Carlos used to visit his grandmother in the neighboring town. He called her *Abuelita* (Granny, in Spanish). He loved Abuelita very much. When he went there to visit, she always baked him his favorite foods, and she always gave him just one gift. Carlos didn't know how Abuelita knew, but her gift was always just what he wanted. It was always very special.

When Carlos arrived at Abuelita's house the year he turned six, he began to look all around for his gift. He didn't see any packages around the house. He wondered, "Did Abuelita forget to buy my present?" He ate dinner that night and went to church with Abuelita. After church, he ate two pieces of candy and drank a big glass of milk. He went to bed and dreamed about snow.

The next morning Carlos woke up very early. He jumped out of bed and looked out the window. The ground in front of the house was covered with a blanket of white. Carlos ran downstairs in his pajamas and opened the front door. He stepped out and felt cold, wet stuff. "*¡Nieve!*" (Snow!) he shouted. "*Gracias,*

Abuelita." (Thank you, Granny.) He ran and played in the *nieve* until the hot sun melted it all, which was very soon.

And that was the best Christmas present Carlos remembered for the rest of his life. He never found out that his Abuelita paid a lot of money to the local ice cream company (in Mexico they call ice cream *nieve,* the same word for "snow," but the Spanish word for ice cream is *helado,* which means "frozen") to spread coconut ice cream all over her front yard!

A little note about *Abuelita*: If you add *-ito* or *-ita* to a word in Spanish, it makes that thing smaller, or diminutive. It can be added to nouns as well as adjectives. That's why *Abuelita* means "little grandmother," or "Granny."

Honey, I Shrunk the World!

Make the following Spanish nouns diminutive by chopping off the last letter and adding *-ito* or *-ita.* (Remember the masculine and feminine endings!) Then write what they mean in English.

muchacho _____

pato _____

sombrero _____

Lola _____

Pablo _____

➥ *Answers are at the end of the chapter.*

Now go back to the story about snow and underline or highlight all the verbs.

Not Perfectly Past Verbs

Did you notice that the verbs in the first two paragraphs—the ones describing Carlos, telling of his daily activities, what he used to do, or always did, like a routine or repeated actions each day—are very different from the tone of the rest of the story? Once the story shifts to "When Carlos arrived at Abuelita's house the year . . . ," the verbs are in the preterite, like in Poor Pablo's story. The first two paragraphs are not really *perfectly* in the past, not like they would be in the preterite. If you were to plot these verbs on a time line, you would have a hard time pinpointing exactly when Carlos did all that. However, as soon as he arrived at Abuelita's house, it is easy to put his actions on a time line.

This verb form in the past is called the *imperfect past tense,* or the imperfect preterite. The imperfect is always a description in the past, or a repeated or continuous action, something you used to do, or two actions going on at the same time in the past.

Perfectly Preterite or Imperfect?

Write a **P** next to the preterite verbs and an **I** next to the imperfect verbs.

1. ___ I used to go.
2. ___ He went.
3. ___ The birds were singing.
4. ___ They slept.
5. ___ Carlos won.
6. ___ He bought.

7. ___ Carlos ran.
8. ___ Carlos was six.
9. ___ Carlos used to go.
10. ___ We laughed.
11. ___ I used to jog.
12. ___ Did you go?

13. ___ Pablo ate.
14. ___ She sang.
15. ___ They saw.
16. ___ We were dancing.
17. ___ They said.
18. ___ I didn't find it.

➧ *See the answers at the end of the chapter.*

Don't Forget About *Ían* and *Aban!*

If you were walking down a dark alley in Mexico City, and a couple of thugs, named Ían and Aban, the slimy, imperfect verb endings, bumped into you and knocked you over, do you know how the police would immediately know their names? *Because imperfect verb endings always have an -ían or an -aban in their name!*

Gosh! Does that mean that for the verbs *preferir, decidir, vender, tener, dominar, explorar,* the imperfect verb ending for these two thugs would be *preferían, decidían, vendían, tenían, dominaban, exploraban*? SURE ENOUGH! The -*er* and -*ir* verbs have the -*ían* ending, and the -*ar* verbs have the -*aban* ending. At least, they do in the **third-person plural**, which is *ellos, ellas, ustedes*.

For the first- and third-person singular, simply **take off the letter n**: *prefería, decidía, vendía, tenía, dominaba, exploraba*. And just add *s* for the second-person singular: *preferías, decidías, vendías, tenías, dominabas, explorabas*. The first-person plural has the familiar -*amos*, which is reminiscent of the present tense as well as the preterite. So the whole conjugation, just based on *Ían* and *Aban*, would look like this:

IMPERFECT	
-aba	-ía
-abas	-ías
-aba	-ía
-ábamos	-íamos
-aban	-ían

preferir	decidir	vender
prefería	decidía	vendía
preferías	decidías	vendías
prefería	decidía	vendía
preferíamos	decidíamos	vendíamos
prefer**ían**	decid**ían**	vend**ían**

tener	dominar	explorar
tenía	dominaba	exploraba
tenías	dominabas	explorabas
tenía	dominaba	exploraba
teníamos	dominábamos	explorábamos
ten**ían**	domin**aban**	explor**aban**

Dos Excepciones (Two Exceptions)

For the very curious, or the very self-motivated, there are two very different-looking, very irregular imperfect conjugations for the verbs *ser* and *ir*. The conjugations are:

ser	ir
era	iba
eras	ibas
era	iba
éramos	íbamos
eran	iban

(There are actually three irregular imperfect verbs in the entire Spanish language. The third one is the verb *ver*, "to see," and instead of *vía*, it's conjugated *veía*. Just a tiny change!)

Summary

The imperfect differs from the preterite in that the imperfect tense is used for actions in the past that were continuous, but not completed. The imperfect is used for descriptions (the sun was shining, the birds were singing) or for an activity you used to do in the past (I used to play chess, we used to visit our grandmother), a repeated activity (every Saturday I played basketball), or two activities going on at the same time (he was talking on the phone while I was washing my hair).

The endings in Spanish for the imperfect for *-ar* verbs are: *-aba, -abas, -aba, -ábamos, -aban,* and for *-er* and *-ir* verbs are: *-ía, -ías, -ía, -íamos, -ían.* Two exceptions are *ser* (*era*) and *ir* (*iba*). A third one is *ver* (*veía*).

 Remember to draw a picture in the Contents.

Answers to "Honey, I Shrunk the World!"

muchacho	muchachito, little boy
pato	patito, little duck
sombrero	sombrerito, little hat
Lola	Lolita, little Lola
Pablo	Pablito, little Pablo

Answers to "Perfectly Preterite or Imperfect?"

1. I	7. P	13. P
2. P	8. I	14. P
3. I	9. I	15. P
4. P	10. P	16. I
5. P	11. I	17. P
6. P	12. P	18. P

Que Será Será

Close your eyes and visualize something you really want to have happen. Play some soft baroque music while you have your eyes closed. Breathe slowly and deeply as you begin. See all the details with your mind's eye. Hear the sounds, see the people involved, picture the end result as though it has already happened. When your picture is complete, open your eyes. Welcome back!

Remember this Doris Day song?

"Que será será,
Whatever will be will be,
The **future**'s not ours to see
Que será será"

Maybe 1956 was too long ago for you. Perhaps you can find someone who can sing the tune of this song to you. *Will be* is the *future tense*. Not the present tense, not the past tense, not the preterite nor the imperfect, but the future tense. *I will* or *I shall* is the future tense.

The set of endings for conjugating verbs in the future in Spanish looks a lot like *será*. The future endings all have accent marks too, like the preterite endings. What's different about future tense endings, however, is that you don't need to alter the infinitive with the *-ar, -er, -ir* endings: just leave the infinitive intact. Here's what the first three persons singular look like:

	ser	dominar	responder	decidir
I	seré	dominaré	responderé	decidiré
you	serás	dominarás	responderás	decidirás
he, she, it, you formal	será	dominará	responderá	decidirá

The Cheerleading Game

First, thump the table top or clap your hands as you say the three future tense endings: -é, -ás, -á. They sound like this: **ay, ahss, ah**! Next, pretend you're cheerleading for your favorite team, with pom-poms and all. Jump up and down and sing: "Give me an AY! Give me an AHSS! Give me an AH!" If you know the tune, sing the verb forms to the first couple lines of the song "YMCA!" For example: *¡Do-mi-na-ré!* (It even rhymes with YMCA!) Don't worry if you don't know the song. You can still yell loudly as you swing your arms around, and say the first three persons singular of the future tense using the following verbs:

dominar	admirar	solicitar
ocupar	depositar	plantar
investigar	curar	pasar
observar	cultivar	ordenar
visitar	invitar	transportar
marchar	tolerar	inventar
concentrar	elevar	estudiar
celebrar	explorar	pintar
comprender	responder	vender
dividir	decidir	permitir

Pretty simple, no? The two remaining plural endings are a combination of the present tense endings for -er, -ir verbs and -ar verbs. Do you remember them? They are -emos, -an. *Visitar* becomes *visitaremos, visitarán*; and *responder* becomes *responderemos, responderán*.

For the very curious, here is the entire conjugation of the future tense. If you are truly interested in jump-starting your Spanish class, it's good to see these so you will recognize them when you have to study them.

ser	dominar	comprender	decidir
seré	dominaré	comprenderé	decidiré
serás	dominarás	comprenderás	decidirás
será	dominará	comprenderá	decidirá
seremos	dominaremos	comprenderemos	decidiremos
serán	dominarán	comprenderán	decidirán

Mystery Activity

There are some exceptions to verb conjugations in the future tense. No surprise! The space below here will be filled up by you **in the future**, with the exceptions to future verb conjugations, after you have dived into the next chapter!

I'm Going To . . .

What do **you** say when you talk about tomorrow, next week, next month, the year 2050? How about "I'm going to" ("I'm gonna" or "they're gonna"). In Spanish you can use the verb "to go" (*ir*) just as you do in English. "I'm going to call you tomorrow." "He's going to visit the doctor." "She's going to go on a diet."

Remember *voy, vas, va, vamos, van* (pronounced **boy, bas, ba, bamos, ban**) from Chapter 9 on irregular verbs? All you have to do to express the simple future is to say *voy a* and then the infinitive verb (that is, leave on the *-ar, -er, -ir*).

> I'm going to visit = Voy a visitar
> I'm going to communicate = Voy a comunicar
> I'm going to sell = Voy a vender

Game: Whatcha Gonna Do Now?

Draw a line from the column on the left with English situations to the column on the right with Spanish actions.

1. Movies or the mall?	A. Voy a inventar.
2. I'm on the way to the bank.	B. Voy a comunicar.
3. My yard needs some trees.	C. Voy a decidir.
4. I'm having a birthday party.	D. Voy a adoptar.
5. I have a big test tomorrow.	E. Voy a vender.
6. I have a science project due.	F. Voy a estudiar.
7. I want to get a new puppy.	G. Voy a insistir.
8. I really want my own way.	H. Voy a invitar.
9. I have to make a phone call.	I. Voy a depositar.
10. I'm having a garage sale.	J. Voy a plantar.

➡ *See answers at the end of the chapter.*

Can you get the general idea of these next whole sentences in Spanish? Write the sentences in English on the lines below.

Voy a invitar a Carlos a mi casa.

_____

Voy a depositar pesos mexicanos en el banco.

_____

Voy a plantar flores en el jardín.

_____

Voy a pasar enfrente de la farmacia.

_____

¡Voy a inventar chocolate sin (*without*) calorías!

_____

Voy a comunicarme con (*with*) mi papá.

_____

Voy a llamar (telefonear) a mi mamá.

_____

Voy a usar un cheque en el restaurante.

_____

And finally, how about these trickier verbs?

Voy a ir a la casa de Pablo.

_____

Voy a ser astronauta.

_____

Voy a estar en el hotel a las 3 de la mañana.

_____

Voy a tener 15 años el 8 de septiembre.

¡Fantástico!

 I hope you're still remembering to draw a picture in the Contents!

Answers to "Whatcha Gonna Do Now?"

1 C, 2 I, 3 J, 4 H, 5 F, 6 A, 7 D, 8 G, 9 B, 10 E

Answers to sentences using *voy a*

I'm going to invite Carlos to my house.
I'm going to deposit Mexican pesos in the bank.
I'm going to plant flowers in the garden.
I'm going to pass in front of the pharmacy.
I'm going to invent chocolate without calories!
I'm going to communicate with my dad.
I'm going to call (phone) my mother.
I'm going to use a check in the restaurant.

I'm going to go to Pablo's house.
I'm going to be an astronaut.
I'm going to be in the hotel at 3 A.M.
I'm going to be 15 years old on September 8.

Excuses, Excuses

QUINCE

How many times have you said, "I would if I could," but you couldn't? "I would help you paint your house, but . . . ," "I would really like to go with you, but . . . ," "I would like to come over Saturday night, but . . . ," "I would go to Cancún this winter, but . . . ," "I would sleep in Sunday morning, but. . . ."

There is always a BUT. There is always a CONDITION. This requires a verb tense in Spanish called the *conditional tense*. It begins with *would*. If you had to place *would* somewhere in time, it would not be in the present or past, but in the future.

Paco's Excuses

My friend Paco is the kind of person who always has an excuse for **not** doing something. Pretend you are Paco and fill in the following excuses with a conditional verb or phrase in English:

Example: **I would go** to the movies tonight, but I have to wash my cat.

I would _____ but my grandmother is visiting.

_____ but my dog ate it.

_____ but my little brother tore it up.

_____ but it was already too late.

_____ but my computer got a virus.

_____ but I ran out of money.

The Lottery Game

How many times have you heard people say, "If I won the lottery, I would . . ."? They were using the conditional tense. "If I won the lottery" is the condition, and "I would" requires the conditional. Here are some "if" clauses followed by a verb in the conditional tense.

If I won the lottery, **I would buy** a yacht and sail around the world.
If I were retired, **I would live** by the ocean.
If I lived in Mexico, **I would eat** a lot of tortillas.

What about you? Make up sentences using "if" clauses like the ones above. An "if" clause can't stand on its own as a sentence (If I won the lottery), so make sure you add a **would** clause (I would buy a yacht).

1. If I won the lottery, I would _____

2. _____

3. _____

4. _____

5. _____

Note 1. This *would* is not the same *would* as when we say "When I was a teenager, I would always ask my mom for a second piece of pie." In that sentence, *would* really means "used to" ask for a second piece of pie, so you would use the imperfect tense. **Read this note again slowly to make sure that you got it!**

Note 2. You can use the conditional without using an "if" clause, such as: "You said you would buy me a new car!" (If that question were in Spanish, you would find a "ghost conjunction" lurking around, as you will see in Chapter 17!)

What About Spanish?

Do you recognize these verb endings: *-ía, -ías, -ía, -íamos, -ían?*

If you remembered Ían, that thug who hung out with Aban, and guessed that these are imperfect verb endings, you are correct! If you add the imperfect endings to the infinitive, or unconjugated verb, you will have the ***conditional*** *tense*:

usaría = I would/he, she, it would use
observaría = I would/he, she, it would observe
vendería = I would/he, she, it would sell
recibiría = I would/he, she, it would receive

Can you attach the *tú, nosotros, ellos/ellas/ustedes* endings (*-ías, -íamos, -ían*) to the verbs below?

usar: _____

observar: _____

vender: _____

recibir: _____

➡ *Check the end of the chapter for the answers.*

Exceptions, Always Exceptions!

There are a few exceptions to the rule about using the unadulterated infinitive. One verb that you know, *tener*, becomes **not** *tenería*, but *tendría*. Several others which have an added *d* (and take away an *e* or *i*) are *-go* verbs like *tener* (see flower petal activity in Chapter 9): *poner, salir,* and *venir* become *pondría, saldría,* and *vendría*. Other *-go* verbs subtract a *c* instead of adding a *d*. For example, *hacer* becomes *haría* and *decir* becomes *diría* (note the stem change).

These exceptions also occur in the future tense, covered in the previous chapter. Here is your chance, in a few minutes, to go back and do the "Mystery Activity."

If the future also takes away the *e* or *i* and adds a *d* for *tener, poner, salir,* and *venir,* what would that look like? Can you remember the first line of the cheer from the cheerleader? Ay! (*é*)

Conditional: tendría, pondría, saldría, vendría

Future: tendr___, pondr___, saldr___, vendr___

If you wrote down: *tendré, pondré, saldré, vendré,* you get an Ay! Go back now and write these in the "Mystery Activity," Chapter 14.

Summary of the Conditional Tense

The conditional tense is like the future in the past. If you say, "When I go to Mexico I will buy a big sombrero," that's the future. If you say, "If I went to Mexico, I would buy a big sombrero," that's the conditional. You can tell a conditional verb if it has *would* in it. There is usually a condition, preceded by the word *if.* I would go, I would eat, I would have. We use two verbs to express this in English.

In Spanish the conditional is just one verb. To conjugate the verb, you keep the infinitive intact, as in future tense conjugations: *observar, vender, recibir, ser, ir,* and add the imperfect endings *-ía, -ías, -ía, -íamos, -ían.* The exception to these endings is adding the letter *d* to certain irregular verbs.

Same routine: draw that picture in the Contents!

Answers to conditional verb endings

usar: usarías, usaríamos, usarían
observar: observarías, observaríamos, observarían
vender: venderías, venderíamos, venderían
recibir: recibirías, recibiríamos, recibirían

A VERY SHORT QUIZZIE

This is a review of all the verb tenses covered so far. Each of the balloons below contains a conjugated verb. Simply write under each verb what tense it's in.

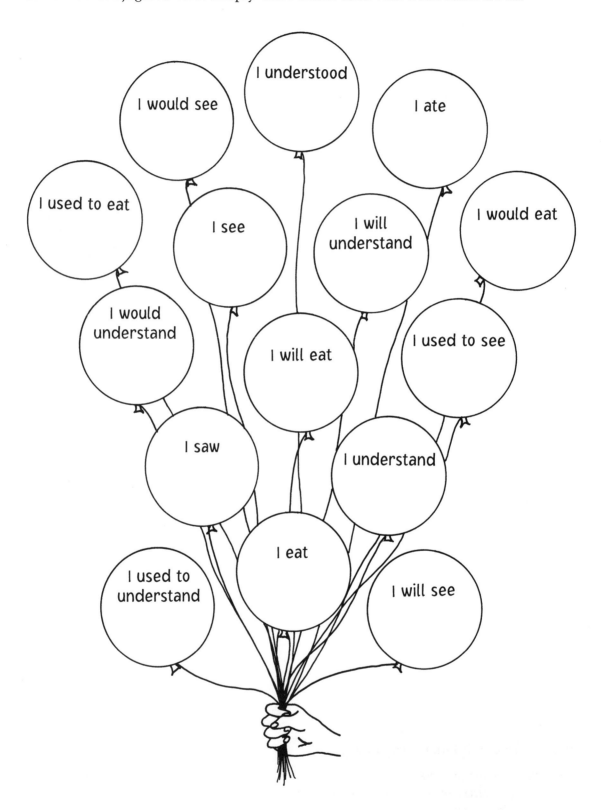

◆ *Answers are on the next page.*

Take A BIG BREAK and have A BIG TREAT!

Answers to "A Very Short Quizzie"

I eat, I see, I understand = present indicative
I ate, I saw, I understood = preterite
I used to eat, I used to see, I used to understand = imperfect
I will eat, I will see, I will understand = future tense
I would eat, I would see, I would understand = conditional tense

What in the World Are You Doing?

Did someone ever say, "What in the world are you doing?" when he or she caught you doing something you shouldn't be doing? Maybe you answered, "I'm brushing your dog's teeth with your toothbrush!" Here are some other more innocent answers: "I'm eating my breakfast." "I'm fixing the car." "I'm painting my toenails." "I'm not doing anything" ("I'm not doing nothing," if you were speaking Spanish).

Eating, doing, painting, brushing, fixing. These verbs all have the same ending: *-ing.* This is the **present participle** ending. It answers the question "What are you do-ing at this moment, right now?"

In Spanish the present participle ending you use is *-ando* or *-iendo* (pronounced **ahn-do** and **yendo**). The first ending is for *-ar* verbs; the second is for *-er* and *-ir* verbs.

usar — usando	vender — vendiendo
celebrar — celebrando	insistir — insistiendo
pintar — pintando	dividir — dividiendo
transportar — transportando	decidir — decidiendo

Let's Be Progressive

The name of the tense that uses the present participle form of the verb, as we learned in Chapter 8, is the *present progressive*. Remember Soylandia and Es-toylandia? Remember *ser* and *estar*? They mean "to be." Look back and see if you can find some more examples of the present progressive in that chapter. The present progressive always uses two verbs; the first is a form of *to be* (*I am*), and the second is the present participle (*doing, brushing, painting,* etc.). Do you remember which verb, *ser* or *estar,* is used in Spanish? If you looked back, you will have found the answer. It's *estar.*

I am painting	Estoy pintando
I am selling	Estoy vendiendo

So, What in the World Are You Doing?

Match the English with the Spanish in the following sentences by drawing a line from the left column to the right column verbs.

Estoy celebrando la Navidad.	I am counting: 1, 2, 3.
Estoy estudiando español.	I am concentrating. Shhh!
Estoy visitando el parque.	I am deciding where I'm going.
Estoy observando los animales.	I am celebrating Christmas.
Estoy inventando una cosa.	I am observing the animals.
Estoy admirando una rosa.	I am visiting the park.
Estoy decidiendo a dónde voy.	I am studying Spanish.
Estoy concentrando. ¡Silencio!	I am inventing something.
Estoy explorando en África.	I am admiring a rose.
Estoy contando: uno, dos, tres.	I am exploring in Africa.

➥ *Answers are at the end of the chapter.*

Now, look at the pictures below, and write, in Spanish, a present participle verb only (with an *-ando* or *-iendo* ending). Here are the verbs you must choose from:

estudiar, vender, admirar, celebrar, contar, visitar, inventar, observar, decidir

Remember *-er* and *-ir* verbs end in *-iendo*!

1. _____

2. _____

3. _____

4. _____

5. _____

6. _____

7. _____

8. _____

9. _____

➡ *Answers are at the end of the chapter.*

The Progressive Imperfect

The progressive imperfect (I was doing) uses the imperfect of *estar*, which is *estaba*, plus the present participle. *Yo estaba estudiando . . . estaba admirando . . . estaba celebrando . . . estaba vendiendo . . . estaba respondiendo.*

Alibi

Pretend there was a robbery at 3 P.M. on September 17, and you have five suspects who were found in the area. They are lined up at the police station. You are going to interview each one to find out whose story is the least believable.

Here are the alibis they give when you ask them, in Spanish, "What were you doing at 3 P.M. on September 17?" Which one is the guilty one? See the end of this chapter for the translation of each alibi and the correct answer!

1. Estaba visitando a mi mamá en el hospital.

   _____

2. Estaba plantando rosas.

   _____

3. Estaba estudiando español en la universidad.

   _____

4. Estaba observando elefantes en un bar.

   _____

5. Estaba vendiendo frutas en el parque.

   _____

 By now, you must be getting good at drawing little pictures in the Contents!

Answers to "So, What in the World Are You Doing?"

Estoy celebrando la Navidad.	I am celebrating Christmas.
Estoy estudiando español.	I am studying Spanish.
Estoy visitando el parque.	I am visiting the park.
Estoy observando los animales.	I am observing the animals.
Estoy inventando una cosa.	I am inventing something.
Estoy admirando una rosa.	I am admiring a rose.
Estoy decidiendo a dónde voy.	I am deciding where I'm going.
Estoy concentrando. ¡Silencio!	I am concentrating. Shhh!
Estoy explorando en África.	I am exploring in Africa.
Estoy contando: uno, dos, tres.	I am counting: 1, 2, 3.

Present participle verbs for the pictures:

1. admirando   2. visitando   3. observando
4. inventando   5. decidiendo   6. contando
7. estudiando   8. celebrando   9. vendiendo

Translation of each alibi

1. I was visiting my mom in the hospital.
2. I was planting roses.
3. I was studying Spanish at the university.
4. I was observing elephants in a bar.
5. I was selling fruit in the park.

Answer: Alibi 4 is the guilty one!

Over the River and Through the Woods

Here is a great eye relaxation. Rub your palms together for a few seconds, then gently place your palms over your eyes, keeping your eyes open. Then uncover your eyes and three times each, look up (arriba) and down (abajo), to the right (derecha) and to the left (izquierda = sounds a little like "he's scared a"). Now diagonally, up and to the right, down and to the left three times. Now circle your eyes clockwise, making a big circle, three times. Do the same counterclockwise. Remove your palms, breathing deeply.

Have you been treating yourself to candy, treats, and bonbons all along the way?

Like bonbons, prepositions and conjunctions are just little, short words.

Prepositions

Prepositions often give the location or position of things.

PREPOSITIONS: to, from, of, on, in, over, under, through, for, with, without

Can you think of any others?

Twinkle, Twinkle, Little Star

In Spanish prepositions are also little, short words. You can even sing your prepositions. Do you know the tune to "Twinkle, Twinkle, Little Star"? Using the tune to the entire song in English, **sing** the following most commonly used Spanish prepositions. Don't sing the English, just repeat the Spanish prepositions for each line of the song.

	Twin	kle	twin	kle	lit	tle	star
(Sing this line.)	**a**	**de**	**en**	**por**	**para**	**con**	**sin**
	to	of	in	through	for	with	without
		from	on	for			

Preposition Hopscotch

Below, two hopscotch games are drawn, one in English and one in Spanish. If you have any dice, throw one on the table and "hop" over the number of squares on the die with your fingertips. Or you can tear up little pieces of paper and write numbers 1–6 on them, place them face down, and choose one at a time. When you land on a square, you must say the prepositions out loud in English then Spanish, or first Spanish then English.

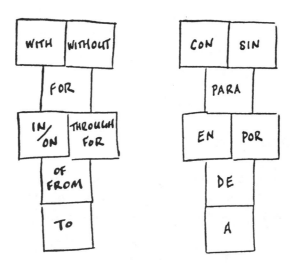

Now play a second time, and make a prepositional phrase using the nouns provided below. A *prepositional phrase* is not a whole sentence, just a preposition and an object of a preposition. For example: *with my sister, on the sofa, in the car.*

my mom	my dad	the car	the house	my friend	the bicycle
mi mamá	mi papá	el carro	la casa	mi amigo	la bicicleta
a duck	the snow	my shoes	the TV	the radio	gasoline
un pato	la nieve	mis zapatos	la tele	la radio	gasolina

Here is an example: you draw or throw a 3, and land on "in/on" or *"en"* and say "in the snow/*en la nieve.*" Then you happen to throw a 2 and land on "for" or *"para"* and say "for my dad/*para mi papá.*" Now it's your turn!

Contractions

Contractions result when you take two words and form one with them. For example: has not = hasn't, do not = don't, is not = isn't.

In the whole Spanish language, can you believe there are only two contractions? They are made from two prepositions, **a** (to) and **de** (from, of).

Al, the contraction of *a + el = al,* and *del, de + el = del.*
Al means "to the," *del* means "from the" or "of the."

> Voy = I go to, I'm going to
> Vengo = I come from, I'm coming from

For example:

Voy **al** banco.	=	I'm going to the bank.
Voy **al** dentista.	=	I'm going to the dentist.
Vengo **del** banco.	=	I'm coming from the bank.
Vengo **del** dentista.	=	I'm coming from the dentist.

The Ghost Preposition

There is a special character, the personal *a.* In English, there is no translation for it! When you say in Spanish, "I observe José," "I admire my dad," or "I visit Carmen in the hospital," you must insert the ghost preposition *a,* called "the personal *a*" before the person you observe, admire, or visit.

For example, the sentences above would be:

> Observo **a** José.
> Admiro **a** mi papá.
> Visito **a** Carmen en el hospital.

So, the personal *a* is actually invisible in English! It's called the personal *a* because it only applies to persons, not things. For example, you say, *Admiro a mi mamá,* but you say *Admiro la rosa.* No personal *a.*

Conjunctions

Conjunctions are "connecting" words, like at the "junction." They are short but very necessary.

CONJUNCTIONS: and, or, but, if, then

Here are the most important conjunctions in Spanish:

o	**y**	**si**	**pero**	**ni**
or	and	if	but	nor

Can you translate this sentence? (Hint: *tiempo* means "time.")

Voy a visitar los elefantes y los tigres en el zoo, pero no los cocodrilos ni las cebras si no tengo tiempo.

➜ *See the end of the chapter for the translation!*

The Ghost Conjunction

There is an invisible ghost conjunction in these sentences in English:

> I think _____ I have learned a lot about Spanish.
> Did you know _____ cats eat birds?
> I believe _____ this chapter is almost finished.

Can you guess what English word could go in each blank? The sentences sound perfectly fine without any conjunction, but in Spanish, you **must** insert . . . the ghost conjunction. It's *that.* In Spanish, you say *que.* Do you remember how to pronounce that? QUE = K.

Ghost Buster Exercise

There are eight ghosts hidden in the sentences below. Even though the sentences are in English, you must be the ghost buster and discover **which** ghost word (the preposition *a* or the conjunction *que*) is missing if the sentence were written in Spanish. You'll also have to figure out **where** the ghost would be in the sentence. When you find the ghost, draw an asterisk (*) and write **A** or **QUE** above it. If you want, you can draw a little ghost around the word!

Like this: I love *my dad. (*The ghost would be the personal* a, *written between the words* love *and* my.)

1. My friend loves his mother very much.

2. I know my cat has fleas.

3. They say people who know another language are more intelligent.

4. Yesterday morning I visited my aunt in the suburbs.

5. We watched a policeman writing out a speeding ticket last week.

6. I believe miracles are around us all the time.

7. We saw the president's wife on television at 10:00.

8. I think learning Spanish will be very easy when I finish this book!

❧ *The answers are at the end of the chapter.*

In the title to this chapter, there are two prepositions and one conjunction. Can you find them?

 Yes, you know, "draw a picture in the Contents."

Answer to sentence with conjunctions

I am going to visit the elephants and the tigers in the zoo, but not the crocodiles or the zebras if I don't have time.

Answers to "Ghost Buster Exercise"

1. My friend loves * (A) his mother very much.
2. I know * (QUE) my cat has fleas.
3. They say * (QUE) people who know another language are more intelligent.
4. Yesterday morning I visited * (A) my aunt in the suburbs.
5. We watched * (A) a policeman writing out a speeding ticket last week.
6. I believe * (QUE) miracles are around us all the time.
7. We saw * (A) the president's wife on television at 10:00.
8. I think * (QUE) learning Spanish will be very easy when I finish this book!

Answer to final question

Prepositions: over, through
Conjunction: and

Eat Your Spinach!

If you think this chapter has something to do with Popeye the Sailorman, it doesn't! It has to do with Popear the Great, the greatest emperor ever to rule Upper Poppover. Popear earned the impressive title of Emperor, or *Imperator* in his language, because he commanded the armies of Upper Poppover, fought valiantly, and won many battles. He was, however, not very well liked by his subjects. Then one Tuesday, everything changed. . . .

The Emperor's Day Off

It was a gloomy day in Upper Poppover. The emperor was more irritable, cranky, and upset than he had ever been.

"I am sick of conquering, pillaging, and plundering week after week. I am especially tired of commanding all day long. I just can't go on any more!" he exclaimed. Then he crawled back into bed, even though it was almost noon, and would not come out of his bedroom.

After several days, Popear's counselors, doctors, and ministers all gathered in the great hall. They had never seen their emperor in such a condition. It was **imperative** that something be done.

A decree was sent out to the entire empire:

THE EMPEROR IS VERY ILL. IF ANYONE CAN COME UP WITH A CURE FOR HIS ILLNESS, THAT PERSON WILL BE REWARDED HANDSOMELY.

The next morning, thousands of people from Upper Poppover filled the courtyards of the royal palace. They carried herbs and potions that were said to cure any ill, but nothing worked. Popear just tossed them out the window into the royal rosebeds.

Finally, a gnarled old woman wearing a brown hooded cape pushed her way through the crowd. She had no basket of herbs, but she held a bony finger high in the air.

"I have the perfect solution!" she cried. "The emperor needs a day off! A day where he doesn't have to command anyone. A day where, instead, he gets to carry out commands!"

The ministers shook their heads. They thought this was a ridiculous solution. But, because there were no others, they decided to approach Popear. They tiptoed up to the royal bedroom where they could hear angry rantings and ravings, moanings and groanings, and shouted the old woman's solution through the closed door.

To everyone's surprise, the door burst open, and the emperor ran down the stairway. "I love that idea! Let's get started today!"

All afternoon the subjects took turns commanding the emperor: "Get on your knees!" "Bow before me!" "Look me in the eyes!" "Bring me your gold!" "Pay your taxes!"

Soon they were bored of the same old commands they had been hearing for so many years and began to add bolder ones: "Scratch my back!" "Tickle my toes!" "Tell me a joke!" "Bring me some pastries!" The counselors looked concerned and turned to see what the emperor would do.

Instead of being angry, Popear was delighted! He carried out each command, giggling all the while. He realized he had not had so much fun since he was a very little boy.

By the end of the afternoon he had decided that from that day on, every Tuesday would be the emperor's day off. And when Popear the Great died, at the age of 123, he was declared the most fun-loving, and most cherished emperor that Upper Poppover had ever had.

This chapter is about the **imperative**. The imperative is the command form. The imperative is a **mood**, not a tense. It's neither present, past, nor future on a time line, because it hasn't happened yet. To help you remember the word "imperative," think of the emperor's commands. Emperor = *Imperator* = imperative.

Authority figures, police officers, parents, and teachers use the imperative a lot. You can use the imperative politely: Please, take your shoes off. Come on in! Make yourself at home.

The Masters and Slaves Game

Think of five commands that the following people might say:

Mom/Dad	**Teacher**
Eat your spinach!	Study!

1. _____ _____

2. _____ _____

3. _____ _____

4. _____ _____

5. _____ _____

Police officer	Aerobics instructor/P.E. teacher
Pull over!	Do push-ups!

1. _____   _____

2. _____   _____

3. _____   _____

4. _____   _____

5. _____   _____

In Spanish, the key to remembering how to form the command or imperative mood is:

"*A* Becomes *E* and *E* Becomes *A*"

That is, *-ar* verbs change to *-e* endings and *-er* and *-ir* verbs change to *-a* endings. This ending change is strictly for the *usted,* or formal, command form. It looks like this:

Infinitive	Imperative (*Ud.* form)	Negative Imperative
dominar	¡Domine!	¡No domine!
visitar	¡Visite!	¡No visite!
comprender	¡Comprenda!	¡No comprenda!
vender	¡Venda!	¡No venda!
insistir	¡Insista!	¡No insista!

If you are commanding more than one person (*ustedes,* "you all"), simply add the letter *-n* to the verb. For example: *domine, dominen; comprenda, comprendan.*

Here is what the *tú* form looks like in the imperative. It helps if you see the negative imperative of the *usted* form first:

Negative Imperative (*Ud.* form)	Negative Imperative (*tú* form)	Positive Imperative (*tú* form)
¡No domine!	¡No domines!	¡Domina!
¡No visite!	¡No visites!	¡Visita!
¡No comprenda!	¡No comprendas!	¡Comprende!
¡No venda!	¡No vendas!	¡Vende!
¡No insista!	¡No insistas!	¡Insiste!

Do you see what happens with the *tú* form? The ending stays the same as in the present tense, i.e., *-ar* verbs end in *-a,* and *-er* and *-ir* verbs end in *-e.* Tricky, eh?

The Billboard Game

You are driving down the road from the Cancún airport to your hotel. It's lined with large signs in Spanish, and you discover that you can read and translate them with ease. What do they say? Make sure you say them out loud, like something you would hear on a television commercial.

¡VISITE ACAPULCO EN SUS VACACIONES!

¡EXPLORE EL DESIERTO KALAHARI EN ÁFRICA!

¡PLANTE ÁRBOLES EN EL PARQUE!

¡USE PASTA DENTAL COLGATE PARA DIENTES BLANCOS!

¡OBSERVE LOS TIGRES, LEONES, Y ELEFANTES EN EL ZOOLÓGICO!

¡ADOPTE UN ANIMAL!

¡DEPOSITE SUS PESOS Y DÓLARES EN EL BANCO NACIONAL!

¡CELEBRE LA NAVIDAD EN CASA CON SU FAMILIA!

¡VENDA SU AUTO EN LA SECCIÓN CLASIFICADA!

➦ *Of course, the answers can be found at the end of the chapter!*

Look Before You Leap!

Way back in Chapter 11, about DOPs and IOPs, there was a reference to using two object pronouns together. It would be helpful to go back and locate that note right now (see page 99). It says that when you are using an order or command such as "Give it to me!" you merge the two object pronouns into a single word: *melo, tela, noslos,* etc. Note that the indirect object pronoun always comes first. Then you must attach the object pronouns to the imperative verb, making a single word of the verb and object or objects. Whether you have one object pronoun with a command or two, you must attach it to the end of the verb.

Please, Please, Please!

Here are some of the commands from The Billboard Game with attached object pronouns. Can you understand these commands or requests?

¡Visíteme!
¡Obsérvalo!
¡Adóptenos!
¡Véndamelos!

➦ *Answers are on the next page.*

Draw a billboard or can of spinach in the Contents!

Answers to "The Billboard Game"

VISIT ACAPULCO ON YOUR VACATION!
EXPLORE THE KALAHARI DESERT IN AFRICA!
PLANT TREES IN THE PARK!
USE COLGATE TOOTHPASTE FOR WHITE TEETH!
OBSERVE THE TIGERS, LIONS, AND ELEPHANTS IN THE ZOO!
ADOPT AN ANIMAL!
DEPOSIT YOUR PESOS AND DOLLARS IN THE NATIONAL BANK!
CELEBRATE CHRISTMAS AT HOME WITH YOUR FAMILY!
SELL YOUR CAR IN THE CLASSIFIED SECTION!

Answers to "Please, Please, Please!"

Visit me! (*usted* form)
Observe it! (*tú* form)
Adopt us! (*usted* form)
Sell them to me! (*usted* form)

19

I Should Have Went ... Oops!

Can you find the error in the title of this chapter? I've heard lots of people say "I should have **went**," or "I could have **went**," or "he must have **went**." Those people must have been absent the day **past participles** were taught in school. Maybe the teachers really planned to teach past participles, but the lesson fell on a snow day! Other common mistakes are "he must have did," "we should have drank," "they might have ate."

Past participles are those verb forms that must be the nightmare of every foreigner who tries to learn English: *drink, drank, **drunk**; eat, ate, **eaten**; see, saw, **seen**; do, did, **done**; fly, flew, **flown**.*

The first verbs in the series—*drink, eat, see, do, fly*—are in the infinitive (like *-ar*, *-er*, and *-ir* ending verbs in Spanish). The second verbs—*drank, ate, saw, did, flew*—are in the past tense (the preterite in Spanish). The third verbs—*drunk, eaten, seen, done, flown*—are the past participles.

This chapter is not meant to teach English past participles, although it's not a bad idea because they are much harder in English than in Spanish! The purpose is simply to show what a past participle is. You can recognize a past participle because it goes with the verb *to have*. For example: *I **have gone**, you **have drunk**, he **has eaten**, she **has seen**, we **have done**, they **have flown**.*

This chapter is also about **compound verb tenses**. They are called *compound* because the verb is composed of two verbs. For example, "I have," called the auxiliary verb, and the past participle, "gone." Compound tenses are the opposite of **simple tenses**, composed of just one verb such as "I observe, they admire, he explored." In Spanish, so far we have been talking about simple verb tenses, the present (*admiro*), the preterite (*admiré*), the imperfect (*admiraba*), the future (*admiraré*), and the conditional (*admiraría*). Some of these tenses, which are just one verb in Spanish, are actually two in English (*did admire, will admire, would admire*). Just in case this is putting you to sleep, it's story time!

The Story of Abear

Many, many years ago, before people walked the earth, there lived
a big, burly, brown bear. His parents had never given him a proper
name, so he was just known as Abear (pronounced ah-**bare**). Abear
had lived for so many years that none of the other bears knew
his real age and therefore considered Abear to be the smartest bear
on earth. He had caught every kind of fish in the lakes, rivers, and
streams of his continent; he had eaten more kinds of berries than
anyone could identify; he had slept in so many caves and lumbered
over so many mountains that he had lost count.

During the long winter, when all the bears hibernated in caves, the baby
bears, who were always very curious, were allowed to give up some of their nap
time in order to ask Abear questions that they had saved up all during spring,
summer, and fall. Even though Abear loved snoozing, he was flattered by the
attention, so he tried to stay awake as long as he could. The minute he sat down
in the cave, the little bears surrounded him and started in at once: "Have you ever
been lost?" "Have you ever caught a fish that was so big you couldn't eat it?"
"Have you ever found poisonous berries in the woods?" "Have you ever seen a
white polar bear?" "Have you ever had a fight with a cheetah?" "Have you ever
rolled head over heels down a grassy hill?" "Have you ever found a mountain that
was too high to climb?" "Have you ever seen the ocean?" And, one at a time, Abear
would answer the questions until he was yawning so much that his mouth began
to look like a big pink cave because Abear was so old he had lost most of his teeth.
Then the little bears would start yawning too, because they couldn't help it,
and pretty soon all the bears would be asleep and snoring until spring arrived.

If this last story hasn't put you to sleep, go back and underline or highlight all the
verbs preceded by *have*.

When you have finished, go back and underline or highlight all the verbs preceded
by *had*.

The verbs preceded by *have* are in the present perfect, and the ones preceded by
had are in the pluperfect.

My Exciting Life!

What are five things you have done in your life that were very adventurous or exciting? Have you ever been on a safari in Africa? Or have you been scuba diving or snorkeling? Have you ever walked on hot coals? Or have you eaten snails? List them below.

1. _____

2. _____

3. _____

4. _____

5. _____

Back to Abear

For the verb that accompanies the past participle (*gone, drunk, eaten, seen, done, flown*), you use *haber* (sounds like ah-**bare**), which is usually only conjugated fully when accompanied by a past participle. *Haber* is the "auxiliary verb"—it changes according to who is doing the action, while the past participle stays the same. The conjugation, in the present, looks like this:

he (pronounced **ay**, as in *pay*)
has (pronounced **ahss**)
ha (Open wide and say **ah**!)
hemos (sounds like **ay**-mohss)
han (like **ahn**)

ay ahss ah
aymohss ahn

Can you say them all together: *Ay, ahss, ah, aymohss, ahn.* Again! *Ay, ahss, ah, aymohss, ahn.* Once again, pretend you're a cheerleader, so yell out these endings and do a cartwheel or big jump at the end! Although these endings don't look like them, they sound just like the future tense verb endings (on page 114). Check them out!

Using the Verb *Haber*

To make a sentence in the present perfect—for example, "I have eaten," "I have gone," or "I have drunk"—you just use *he* (**ay**) plus the past participle of the verb.

Well, you must be saying, how do I know what the past participle of the verb looks like? ***Pan comido!*** (Piece of cake!) Just remove the ending of the infinitive (*-ar, -er, -ir*) and add *-ado* for *-ar* verbs and *-ido* for *-er* and *-ir* verbs. For example:

comunicar	he comunic**ado**
observar	he observ**ado**
usar	he us**ado**
comprender	he comprend**ido**
vender	he vend**ido**
recibir	he recib**ido**

Jamás, Jamás, Jamás (Never, Never, Never)

Now, let's try using the present perfect in Spanish. The word *jamás* means "never." In this game, we will use the double negative: *no he . . . jamás. Jamás* sounds like **ha-mahss**. (The other word for "never" is *nunca,* which you learned in Chapter 7.)

Start by saying: *I have never,* and translate the following into English:

No he invitado jamás	I have never invited.
No he plantado jamás	_____
No he decidido jamás	_____
No he inventado jamás	_____
No he estudiado jamás	_____
No he insistido jamás	_____
No he pensado jamás	_____
No he preferido jamás	_____

➡ *See the answers at the end of the chapter.*

The Pluperfect: More Perfect than Perfect

Consider that to have the imperfect, "I used to go," you must first have the opposite, the perfect: "I went." "I went" is the preterite. It's the perfectly past action. To make a verb more past than past, or more perfect than perfect, you use the *pluperfect.* "He had climbed, he had caught, I had given"—all are the pluperfect.

For example: He climbed Mt. Kilimanjaro last year, but he had climbed Mt. Everest the year before.

In Spanish you form the pluperfect by using a form of *haber* in the imperfect tense plus the past participle of the verb.

había comunicado (comprendido, preferido)	[ah-**bee**-ah]
habías comunicado (comprendido, preferido)	[ah-**bee**-ahss]
había comunicado (comprendido, preferido)	[ah-**bee**-ah]
habíamos comunicado (comprendido, preferido)	[ah-**bee**-ah-mohss]
habían comunicado (comprendido, preferido)	[ah-**bee**-ahn]

In English, these examples would be

I **had** communicated (understood, preferred)
you **had** communicated (understood, preferred)
he, she, it, you **had** communicated (understood, preferred)
we **had** communicated (understood, preferred)
they, you all **had** communicated (understood, preferred)

Any Irregularities?

Of course, there are some irregular past participles, but that's no news. There are always irregularities. No rule is perfect! The Appendix lists some irregular past participles.

¡Ay! ¡Ay! ¡Ay!

Haber is also used in the expression "there is" or "there are" in Spanish.
For example:

There is a funny smell in the garage.
There are bugs crawling around my kitchen.

In Spanish it's a simple word: *hay.* Pronounced like the Spanish exclamation *¡Ay!*

See if you can understand these sentences:

Hay insectos en mi casa.
No hay chocolate en el supermercado.
En el zoológico hay animales fascinantes.

➡ *Check your answers at the end of the chapter.*

Haber vs. Tener

In case you were wondering about whether *haber* can be used for "to have" (to hold or possess), which we learned as *tener* in Chapter 8, the answer is NO! *Haber* is strictly an auxiliary verb used in making compound tenses, and for *hay.*

In this space, draw a fat, furry bear and write everything you've learned in Chapter 19 on his tummy.

 The penultimate time you're asked to draw a picture in the Contents!

Answers to *"Jamás, Jamás, Jamás"*

I have never invited
I have never planted
I have never decided
I have never invented
I have never studied
I have never insisted
I have never thought
I have never preferred

Answers to *"¡Ay! ¡Ay! ¡Ay!"*

There are insects in my house.
There is no chocolate at the supermarket.
At the zoo, there are fascinating animals.

Star Light, Star Bright

Do you ever wish on the first star? Wishing and hoping are things we all do. Close your eyes and wish for something to come true. Breathe slowly and deeply, so you are in a relaxed state as you begin this chapter.

Do you know someone who might write a passage like this one in a diary?

Dear Diary: I hope Cindy comes over to my house tonight. She wants me to go to the mall with her. It's really important for us to see all the kids there. I really hope Jim asks me to the dance Saturday. Mom doesn't want me to go out with him. I just tell her to mind her own business. Then she asks me to iron her clothes and cook dinner. I'm glad that my mom has a job. I hope she gets that raise. She tells me to study hard so I can go to college. I really hope I pass my chemistry test tomorrow. I'm going to ask the teacher to make the questions easy. Cindy wants me to let my hair grow out so that she can perm it for me. I hope Jim talks to me in chemistry. I'm glad he's in all my classes. I hope he sits by me at lunch.

Now read through the same passage noticing the words in bold type:

I hope Cindy **comes over** to my house tonight. She wants me **to go** to the mall with her. It's really important for us **to see** all the kids there. I really hope Jim **asks** me to the dance Saturday. Mom doesn't want me **to go out** with him. I just tell her **to mind** her own business. Then she asks me **to iron** her clothes and **cook** dinner. I'm glad that my mom **has** a job. I hope she **gets** that raise. She tells me **to study** hard so I **can** go to college. I really hope I **pass** my chemistry test tomorrow. I'm going to ask the teacher **to make** the questions easy. Cindy wants me **to let** my hair grow out so that she **can** perm it for me. I hope Jim **talks** to me in chemistry. I'm glad **he's** in all my classes. I hope he **sits** by me at lunch.

If this passage were in Spanish, all the verbs that are in bold type would not be in the present indicative. The verbs in "Dear Diary" look like the present indicative, but you are being fooled! In Spanish they would be in the present *subjunctive*. The subjunctive is a mood, not a tense. It's like wishing on a star, but you can't really plot it on a time line unless it comes true, in which case, it would be in the present indicative.

> The subjunctive is a mood, not a tense.

There are three moods in Spanish—the indicative, the imperative, and the subjunctive.

The key to knowing whether a verb should be in the present indicative (positive and definite) or the present subjunctive (dubious and uncertain) is to notice what comes **before it**. Let's make a list:

I hope . . . She wants me to . . . It's important that . . . I really hope . . . Doesn't want me to . . . I tell her to . . . She asks me to . . . I'm glad . . . I hope . . . I doubt . . . She tells me to . . . so I can . . . I really hope . . . I'm going to ask her to . . . Cindy wants me to . . . so that she . . . I hope . . . I hope

That's a lot of

- wishing
- hoping
- telling or asking
- doubting
- wanting someone to
- feelings (I'm glad that)
- impersonal phrases (it's important that)

In Spanish you use the subjunctive mood when there is a subject change: **I** want **you** to go, **she** wants **me** to, **we** tell **them** to, **you** ask **me** to, **it's** important that **you** do something.

Note that all these expressions come **before** the subjunctive verb, and therefore let you know that you should conjugate the verbs **following them** in the subjunctive.

Executive Musings

Now search for and highlight all the verbs that should be in the subjunctive if this second passage were in Spanish:

I hope we have a good business planning meeting. It's important that everyone show up. I want my staff to review all these notes for the meeting. I'll ask them to stay late. My wife (husband) always tells me to come home on time for dinner so the family can spend some time together. I'm glad she (he) shops and cooks part of the time. I tell her (him) to send out for pizza or Chinese. I hope the doctor tells me my cholesterol is low, and that my heart is OK. It's important that I stay fit.

➥ *See the answers at the end of the chapter.*

Recognition and Formation

The best thing about the present subjunctive is that it is almost like the present indicative. Just a few letter switches. *A* **becomes** *e*, and *e* **becomes** *a*!

Take an *-ar* verb like *explorar*, "to explore." Instead of having the first person (I/*yo*) end in *-o*, as all regular verbs do in the present tense, it ends in *-e*: *explore*. And an *-er* verb like *comprender*, "to understand," ends in *-a*: *comprenda*. The *-ir* verbs also end in *-a*.

That's all you need to remember for now about forming the subjunctive endings:

A **becomes** *e*, and *e* **becomes** *a*!

Déjà Vu?

If this is sounding like something you've heard before, you must have been paying attention. There **is** another verb mood that uses the same formula, "*a* becomes *e*, *e* becomes *a*." It's the imperative or command from Chapter 18, *¡Explore! ¡Comprenda!* The difference is that with the present subjunctive, you conjugate the entire verb just as you would any other verb, in all the persons from *yo* to *ustedes*.

By now, you must be dying of curiosity to see what a present subjunctive verb looks like, compared to a present indicative one. Just look below:

explorar		comprender	
Indicative	**Subjunctive**	**Indicative**	**Subjunctive**
exploro	explore	comprendo	comprenda
exploras	explores	comprendes	comprendas
explora	explore	comprende	comprenda

And there you have it! If you weren't dying of curiosity, you should have closed your eyes! The -ir verb endings are exactly the same as the -er verb endings.

Can you fill in the verb *decidir*?

decidir

Indicative	Subjunctive
_____	_____
_____	_____
_____	_____

➡ *Answers are at the end of the chapter.*

The Missing Persons

Just in case you want to figure out what the last two persons in the plural are, try to guess! If you remember -ar verbs have an *e,* and -er and -ir verbs have an *a,* what do you think *exploramos/exploran* and *comprendemos/comprenden* (in the present indicative) would be in the subjunctive? You probably guessed it: *exploremos/exploren* and *comprendamos/comprendan.*

Follow Through!

Now, **you** write in the entire verb conjugation for the present subjunctive.

explorar	comprender	decidir
_____	_____	_____
_____	_____	_____
_____	_____	_____
_____	_____	_____
_____	_____	_____

➡ *See the end of the chapter for the answers.*

Using the Subjunctive

Knowing when to use the subjunctive comes with practice. When you say in English "I want her to do this," what you're actually saying in Spanish is "I want that she does this."

Oh Que!

The word *que* ("that") is very important, and it almost **always** precedes a verb in the subjunctive. In fact, it's like a "tip-off" word. When you conjugate the verb, you should start with *que*: *que yo explore, que tú explores, que él explore,* etc.

If you don't remember ghost conjunctions from Chapter 17, you might want to look back and check.

Christmas Wishes

Write in the space provided all the things you hope that the people in your life will give you: your mom or dad, your boss, your teacher, your brother or sister, your best friend, your wife or husband. You can also make altruistic wishes, such as world peace.

Examples:

> I hope my teacher gives me an A in Spanish.
> I want everyone in the world to stop fighting and just love one another.
> I hope Santa brings me a Jaguar for Christmas.

1. _____

2. _____

3. _____

4. _____

5. _____

6. _____

Now go back to your Christmas wishes and highlight every verb that would be in the subjunctive in Spanish.

An Exception

What do you want for yourself for Christmas? In Spanish, if you have the same subject, for example, "I want to go to Mexico on vacation," or "I hope to visit the Taj Mahal," you would NOT use the subjunctive. If there is no subject change, you simply use the infinitive, in these examples "to go" (*ir*) and "to visit" (*visitar*).

Before the next exercise, draw a big star here, and inside it write key words that will help you remember everything you know about the subjunctive mood. Go back to the beginning of the chapter if you need to.

The Ideal Person

Complete the following:

I want my ideal wife, husband, friend, boyfriend, girlfriend, partner (pick one) to:

_____

_____

_____

_____

_____

_____

_____

_____

Again, highlight all the verbs that would be in the subjunctive in Spanish.

Here's what my ideal partner would be like:

I want my ideal partner to do the laundry. I want him to do all the vacuuming and to load the dishes in the dishwasher. I want him to bring me flowers and hug me and kiss me. I want him to hold hands with me in the movies. I want him to love dancing. I want him to be good-looking. I want him to be in great physical shape. I want him to have a wonderful sense of humor.

Here are the verbs that I highlighted:

I want my ideal partner **to do** the laundry. I want him **to do** all the vacuuming and **to load** the dishes in the dishwasher. I want him **to bring** me flowers and **hug** me and **kiss** me. I want him **to hold** hands with me in the movies. I want him **to love** dancing. I want him **to be** good-looking. I want him **to be** in great physical shape. I want him **to have** a wonderful sense of humor.

Ser and *Ir*

The subjunctive forms of the verbs *ser* and *ir* are irregular. You didn't think we would end this chapter without mentioning irregularities, did you?

> The present subjunctive of *ser*: sea, seas, sea, seamos, sean
> The present subjunctive of *ir*: vaya, vayas, vaya, vayamos, vayan

Perhaps you've heard the popular song or expression *Vaya con Dios* ("Go with God").

Go, Verbs!

The present subjunctive of -*go* verbs is similar to the first person in the present indicative:

> tener: tenga, tengas, tenga, tengamos, tengan
> venir: venga, vengas, venga, vengamos, vengan

Postscript

There is a past subjunctive in Spanish, but you will have to learn about it in a very advanced Spanish class!

Summary of the Subjunctive

The subjunctive is an uncertain verb mood. It's about doubt. It's about wishes and possibilities, not actual facts. You can tell a subjunctive by phrases that precede it, such as: *I want, I wish, I hope, it's possible that, it's uncertain, it's important.* Also by expressions of emotion, like *I'm happy that* and *I'm sorry that.*

Here is how you would say these expressions in Spanish (note the presence of the ghost conjunction *que*):

> I want: quiero que

> I wish: Ojalá que (this expression comes from the Arabic word *Allah*)

> I hope: espero que

> It's possible that: Es possible que

> It's necessary that: Es necesario que

> It's important that: Es importante que

> I'm happy that: Me alegro que

> I'm sorry that: Siento que

In Spanish, subjunctive verbs in the present are the opposite of present indicative tense verbs (*-ar* verbs to *a*; *-er, -ir* verbs to *e* or *i*). Instead, they follow the rule:

> *-ar* verbs change to *e* endings (*admire, admires, admire, admiremos, admiren*)

> *-er, -ir* verbs change to *a* endings (*venda, vendas, venda, vendamos, vendan; decida, decidas, decida, decidamos, decidan*)

The "tip-off" word for the subjunctive is *que*. It usually precedes any verb conjugated in the subjunctive mood.

 Don't let your joy at finishing the final lesson allow you to forget to draw that picture in the Contents!

Answers to "Executive Musings"

The highlighted verbs should be: **we have, show up, to review, to stay, to come, can, shops, cooks, to send, tells, stay.**

Answers to "Déjà Vu?"

decido, decides, decide; decida, decidas, decida

Answers to "Follow Through!"

explorar	comprender	decidir
explore	comprenda	decida
explores	comprendas	decidas
explore	comprenda	decida
exploremos	comprendamos	decidamos
exploren	comprendan	decidan

EXTRA-CREDIT REVIEW QUIZZIE

This is a review of all the verb tenses and moods studied in this book. Match up the column on the left with the column on the right by drawing a line, pairing the Spanish verb with the translation.

1. planté   a. I would plant

2. planto   b. I planted

3. plantaré   c. I am planting

4. he plantado   d. I'm going to plant

5. plantar   e. I will plant

6. plantaban   f. Plant!

7. plantaría   g. I plant

8. voy a plantar   h. they used to plant

9. ¡Plante!   i. that I plant

10. que yo plante   j. I have planted

11. estoy plantando   k. to plant

Answers

1 b, 2 g, 3 e, 4 j, 5 k, 6 h, 7 a, 8 d, 9 f, 10 i, 11 c

A FUN FINAL EXAM

Here is a review of everything you have learned in all the chapters in Sections Two and Three. Have fun!

Directions

A. Play relaxing, preferably baroque, music. Stop! *¡Es importante!*

B. Read over the words inside the shapes, then figure out the significance or importance of each one.

C. Write inside each shape something that will make you remember why these are important, a clue or "trigger." You may want to look up anything you are not sure of. The Glossary at the end of the book will help if you're stumped.

D. Color all the shapes to make the most beautiful painting you have ever made! Have fun, and be very proud of yourself. You have made your quick-start into the Spanish language!

➡ *Possible answers are in the Appendix.*

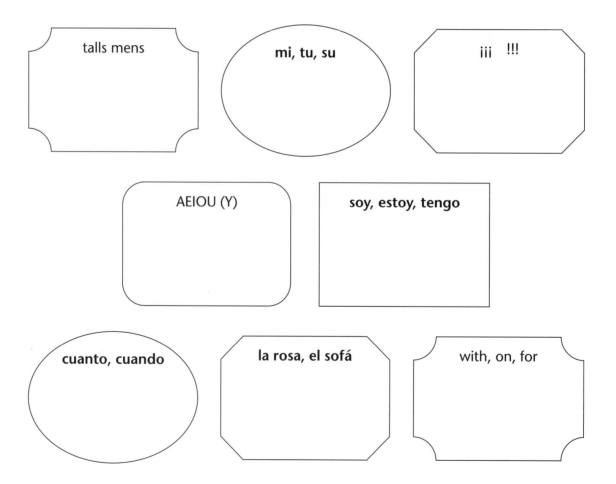

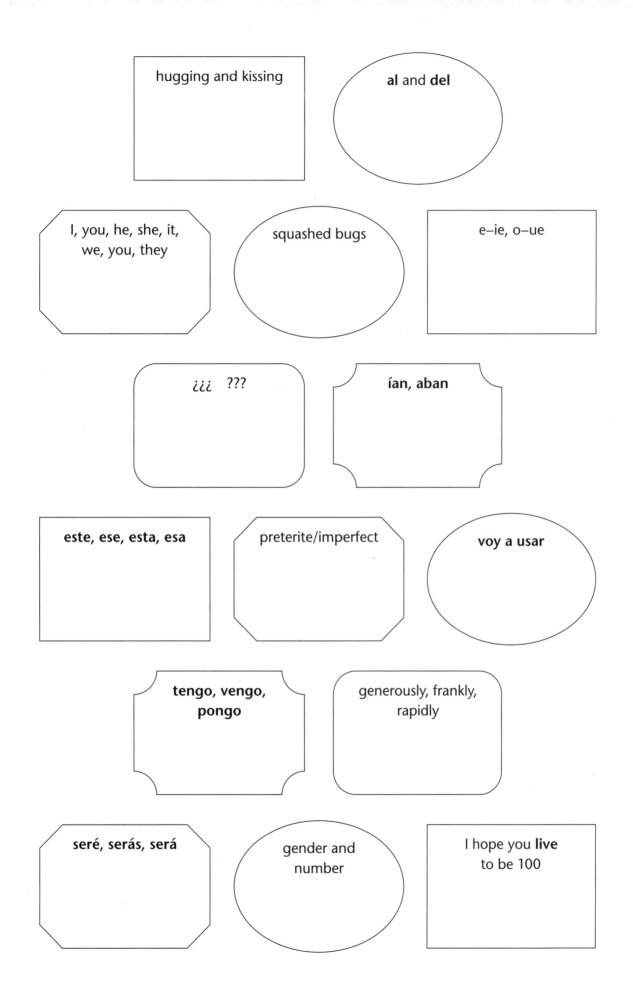

hugging and kissing

al and **del**

I, you, he, she, it, we, you, they

squashed bugs

e–ie, o–ue

¿¿¿ ???

ían, aban

este, ese, esta, esa

preterite/imperfect

voy a usar

tengo, vengo, pongo

generously, frankly, rapidly

seré, serás, será

gender and number

I hope you **live** to be 100

el, la, los, las

-é, -ó

Abear

cuál, cuál

me llamo

-o, -as, -a

¿Qué-Cómo-Mande?

domino, dominas, domina

boy, oh boy

pero, y, o, si

a lake in Italy

Oh ce can you ci?

diphthong

DOPs and IOPs

wishing
and hoping

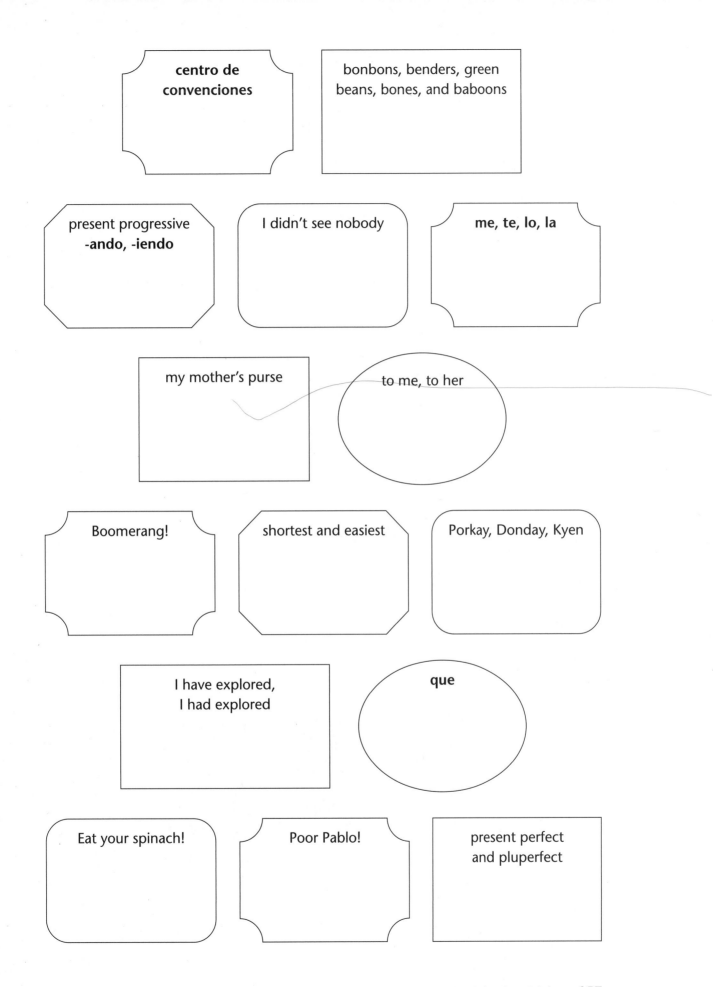

centro de convenciones

bonbons, benders, green beans, bones, and baboons

present progressive -ando, -iendo

I didn't see nobody

me, te, lo, la

my mother's purse

to me, to her

Boomerang!

shortest and easiest

Porkay, Donday, Kyen

I have explored, I had explored

que

Eat your spinach!

Poor Pablo!

present perfect and pluperfect

piña, mañana

A–E
E–A

A kel

hay

jamás

ghosts

cats are furry

hopscotch

Abuelita

If I won the lottery, I'd travel around the world.

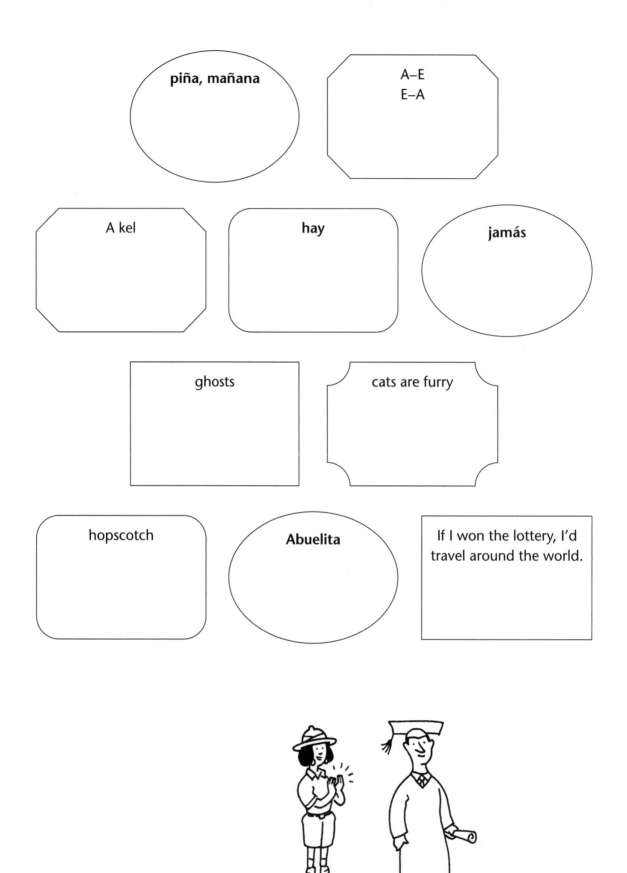

Epilogue

I have a secret to confess. The word that was never mentioned when you began this book was *grammar*. Why? Because many people already have a PFP (Picture from the Past) that it's a boring, terrible, or awful subject. Many teachers dislike teaching English grammar. People tell me things like: "I struggled over diagramming sentences"; "As long as I can talk, who cares about prepositions, adverbs, and direct object pronouns?"; or "I only learned grammar when I took a foreign language class!"

When you arrive on your first day of a foreign language class, your teacher somehow assumes that you know grammar. That you understand personal pronouns, direct object pronouns, verbs, adverbs, nouns, adjectives, etc. You may have studied them, but did you master them well enough to take on grammar in a new language? Probably not! Not until now, since you have finished *Quick-Start Spanish*.

The mysteries of Spanish grammar and pronunciation are clear to you now, not only the concepts but also the logic, the structure behind the words. Sort of like what is behind the TV panel.

Now that you have quick-started Spanish, you can enter any Spanish class and be way ahead of everyone else. Everything will be very clear. And you **WILL** learn easily. Guaranteed!

In case you're wondering, here is what you really learned. You can use this table as a reference in the future. You can also refer to the Glossary at any time to make sure of any terms you don't remember.

Section One

Pronunciation (vowels and consonants, nasal sounds, diphthongs, and accent marks)
Pronunciation games, including cognates

Section Two   Beginner grammar

1 Nouns, articles, gender, and number
2 Noun and adjective agreement
3 Possessive adjectives
4 Demonstrative pronouns and adjectives
5 Personal or subject pronouns

Appendix

Section One: The Yoyo Exercise

monkey	almost	cat	hi
floor	seal	photo	prickly pear
steps on	weight	a well	eyeglasses
child	bathtub	duck	crib
a step	clown	arrives	paw
toad	hand	year	leaf
bear	female bear	uses	night
stick	lime	soup	thread
diver	waiter	boat	popsicle
wine	house	bad	owl
eye	each	nothing	potato (or pope)
headlight	speed bump	cucumber	he plays
shoe	tail	turkey	pineapple
a little	crazy	boy's name	wave
eats	alone	cup	silk
juice	date	map	puma
living room	lagoon	bad (f.)	chicken
hair	pretty	stamp	cuckoo
coat	table	but	a mine
dumb	movies	moon	the letter j
female cat	mommy	daddy	son
smoke	plate	finger	daughter
hour	days	Monday	dough
cap	cow	robe	healthy
meat	wood	life	cousin

Section One: The "What Am I?" Game

ac-**tor**	sen-**si**-ble	in-te-li-**gen**-te	**ra**-dio
te-le-vi-**sión**	po-**si**-ble	pro-**ba**-ble	a-ni-**mal**
dó-lar	co-mer-**cial**	e-le-**gan**-te	e-le-**fan**-te
to-**ma**-te	im-por-**tan**-te	**ta**-xi	i-lu-**sión**
ar-ti-fi-**cial**	co-**lor**	ba-**na**-na	mos-**qui**-to
mo-**tor**	na-tu-**ral**	o-pi-**nión**	po-pu-**lar**
tro-pi-**cal**	**pia**-no	ac-ci-**den**-te	am-bu-**lan**-cia
as-pi-**ri**-na	**mú**-si-ca	pro-fe-**sor**	res-tau-**ran**-te

ho-**tel**	sec-**tor**	**ti**-gre	ca-**fé**
sa-xo-**fón**	**fru**-ta	ga-so-**li**-na	im-po-**si**-ble
ge-ne-**ral**	e-le-**men**-to	e-**fec**-to	per-**so**-na
ci-**vil**	de-ci-**sión**	in-fe-**rior**	su-pe-**rior**
do-cu-**men**-to	**die**-ta	com-**ple**-to	a-pe-**ti**-to
bi-ci-**cle**-ta	ham-bur-**gue**-sa	cri-mi-**nal**	di-fe-**ren**-te
pro-**ble**-ma	ba-**llet**	mu-si-**cal**	den-**tal**
mon-**ta**-ña	far-**ma**-cia	**ne**-gro	as-tro-**nau**-ta
gui-**ta**-rra	**fút**-bol	**te**-nis	**golf**
pro-**gra**-ma	**sand**-wich	li-mo-**na**-da	u-**sual**
i-le-**gal**	or-di-**na**-rio	nor-**mal**	se-cre-**ta**-ria
i-ni-**cial**	**au**-to	mo-**der**-no	tra-di-cio-**nal**
de-**mó**-cra-ta	pre-si-**den**-te	car-pin-**te**-ro	ca-len-**da**-rio
co-**rrec**-to	fa-**ná**-ti-co	cha-cha-**chá**	**fo**-to
dic-cio-**na**-rio	a-me-ri-**ca**-no	tu-**ris**-ta	**ta**-co
mo-**men**-to	te-**lé**-fo-no	ex-cur-**sión**	in-ven-**tor**
doc-**tor**	den-**tis**-ta	vol-**cán**	au-to-**bús**
len-**gua**-je	es-truc-**tu**-ra	e-fec-**ti**-vo	

es**pa**cio	escor**pión**	reli**gio**so	lib**eral**
computa**dora**	sentim**ental**	ro**mán**tico	fa**moso**
banco	dina**mita**	fabu**loso**	cues**tión**
sinfo**nía**	ginecolo**gía**	**ra**ro	espe**cial**
deli**cio**so	cris**tal**	posi**tivo**	nega**tivo**
a**ná**lisis	mis**te**rio	miste**rio**so	cu**rio**so
maravi**lloso**	ape**tito**	pre**cioso**	reli**gión**
protes**tante**	ca**tólico**	pi**rá**mide	**rui**na
di**ná**mico	**mon**struo	es**tú**pido	pro**gra**ma
calmo	**clá**sico	fan**tás**tico	es**quí**

Word Meanings

space	scorpion	religious	liberal
computer	sentimental	romantic	famous
bank	dynamite	fabulous	question
symphony	gynecology	rare	special
delicious	crystal	positive	negative
analysis	mystery	mysterious	curious
marvelous	rapid	precious	religion
protestant	catholic	pyramid	ruin
dynamic	monster	stupid	program
calm	classic	fantastic	ski

Chapter 6: English Meanings (Domino Game)

Group One

I dominate	I admire	I solicit
I occupy	I deposit	I plant
I research	I opt	I cure
I observe	I cultivate	I calm
I order	I conspire	I visit
I pass	I command	I invite
I mark	I transport	I need
I march	I tolerate	I invent
I concentrate	I elevate	I liberate
I celebrate	I explore	I paint
I cooperate	I adopt	I cause
I examine	I continue	I pronounce
I install	I interpret	I calculate

Group Two

I sell	I comprehend	I respond (answer)

Group Three

I describe	I insist	I decide

Chapter 9: Stem-Changing Verbs

Here is the whole conjugation for stem-changing verbs:

e–ie	e–ie	e–ie	e–ie	e–ie
prefiero	pienso	cierro	comienzo	siento
prefieres	piensas	cierras	comienzas	sientes
prefiere	piensa	cierra	comienza	siente
preferimos	pensamos	cerramos	comenzamos	sentimos
prefieren	piensan	cierran	comienzan	sienten

e–ie	e–ie	o–ue	o–ue	u–ue
entiendo	despierto	cuesto	almuerzo	juego
entiendes	despiertas	cuestas	almuerzas	juegas
entiende	despierta	cuesta	almuerza	juega
entendemos	despertamos	costamos	almorzamos	jugamos
entienden	despiertan	cuestan	almuerzan	juegan

o–ue	o–ue	o–ue	o–ue
acuesto	vuelvo	puedo	muero
acuestas	vuelves	puedes	mueres
acuesta	vuelve	puede	muere
acostamos	volvemos	podemos	morimos
acuestan	vuelven	pueden	mueren

Chapter 12: Irregular Preterite Verbs

Here is the whole conjugation of those silly-looking verbs.

Venir (to come)	**Querer** (to want)	**Poner** (to put)	**Poder** (to be able to)
vine	quise	puse	pude
viniste	quisiste	pusiste	pudiste
vino	quiso	puso	pudo
vinimos	quisimos	pusimos	pudimos
vinieron	quisieron	pusieron	pudieron

Saber (to know)	**Hacer** (to make/do)	**Ir/Ser** (to go/to be)
supe	hice	fui
supiste	hiciste	fuiste
supo	hizo	fue
supimos	hicimos	fuimos
supieron	hicieron	fueron

Tener (to have)	**Estar** (to be)
tuve	estuve
tuviste	estuviste
tuvo	estuvo
tuvimos	estuvimos
tuvieron	estuvieron

Chapter 19: Irregular Past Participles

volver (to return): vuelto   decir (to say): dicho

hacer (to make, do): hecho   poner (to put): puesto

Past participles (both regular and irregular) are used to form compound tenses.
For the perfect tenses, a form of *haber* ("to have") is followed by a past participle.

Present perfect		**Pluperfect**	
he vuelto	I have returned	**había vuelto**	I had returned
has hecho	you have made	**habías hecho**	you had made
ha dicho	he has said	**había dicho**	he had said
hemos puesto	we have put	**habíamos puesto**	we had put

A Fun Final Exam (Possible answers)

talls mens

adjective before noun; plural noun, plural adj.

mi, tu, su

mine, yours, his; (possessive adjs.)

iii !!!

exclamation marks before and after

AEIOU (Y)

Spanish vowels; ah, eh, ee, oh, oo, ee

soy, estoy, tengo

three verbs for "to be"; permanence, location, age, hungry, cold, etc.

cuanto, cuando

2 Chinese brothers: how much, when

la rosa, el sofá

fem., masc. articles; mean "the"

with, on, for

prepositions; **con, en, para**

hugging and kissing

demonstratives (this, that); **este, ese** *(little duck story)*

al and **del**

contractions "to the," "of the"

I, you, he, she, it, we, you, they

personal pronouns

squashed bugs

accent marks in Spanish

e–ie, o–ue

stem-changing verbs

¿¿¿ ???

invert question marks at beginning of sentence

ían, aban

imperfect endings

este, ese, esta, esa

*demonstrative
adjectives;
little duck story*

preterite/imperfect

*past tenses; Pablo
story, Carlos story,
and snow story*

voy a usar

I'm going to use

**tengo, vengo,
pongo**

*"-go" verbs in flower;
I have, I come, I put*

**generously, frankly,
rapidly**

*adverbs, end in
"-mente"*

seré, serás, será

*the future tense;
verb "to be"*

gender and number

*masculine, feminine;
singular, plural*

I hope you **live**
to be 100

the subjunctive mood

el, la, los, las

*articles (the)
masc., fem., pl.*

-é, -ó

*preterite endings;
third person sing.*

Abear

*verb haber; "to have";
perfect tenses*

cuál, cuál

*means "which";
little duck story*

me llamo

*"my name is";
may **yah**-mo;
reflexive verb*

-o, -as, -a

*present endings
-ar verbs*

¿Qué-Cómo-Mande?

*ways to say "what?";
Mande is used in
Mexico*

**domino, dominas,
domina**

*present tense of the
-ar verb dominar*

boy, oh boy

*voy, "I'm going";
irregular verb ir*

pero, y, o, si

*conjunctions;
but, and, or, if*

a lake in Italy

Como ("how"/"what")

Oh ce can you ci?

rule about ce, ci (s);
national anthem

diphthong

two vowels together;
io, au, ei, ua

DOPs and IOPs

direct and indirect
object pronouns

wishing
and hoping

subjunctive mood

**centro de
convenciones**

convention center

bonbons, benders, green
beans, bones, and baboons

an, en, in, on, un
pronunciation

present progressive
-ando, -iendo

-ing, going, doing

I didn't see nobody

double negative
in Spanish

me, te, lo, la

Spanish DOPs;
me, you, him, her

my mother's purse

the purse of my
mother; possessive

to me, to her

indirect object
pronouns (IOPs)

Boomerang!

reflexive verb;
to wash yourself

shortest and easiest

superlative adjectives;
the most short, the
most easy

Porkay, Donday, Kyen

why, where, who
¿por qué? ¿dónde?
¿quién?

I have explored,
I had explored

compound tenses; present
perfect and pluperfect

que

"tip-off" word for
the subjunctive to
follow; "that"

Eat your spinach!

Imperative command form

Poor Pablo!

preterite tense time line

present perfect and pluperfect

I have, I had seen; story of Abear

piña, mañana

sounds like "onion"

A–E
E–A

subjunctive endings

A kel

Aquel ("that over there"); demonstrative adjective

hay

"there is," "there are"; haber

jamás

"never"; double negative

ghosts

preposition a; conjunction que

cats are furry

the cats are furry

hopscotch

conjunctions; prepositions

Abuelita

"Granny"; diminutive

If I won the lottery, I'd travel around the world.

conditional tense, with "if" clause first

Extra Credit Exercises

To review the entire book, try these exercises! The answers are on pages 186–89.

Chapter 1

Write the following articles and nouns in the plural. For example: *la rosa—las rosas*.

1. la banana   _____
2. el pato   _____
3. el apartamento   _____
4. la rana   _____
5. el gato   _____

6. el sofá   _____
7. la muchacha   _____
8. el sombrero   _____
9. la niña   _____
10. el carro   _____

How about five more? Be careful! These are slightly different!

11. el actor   _____
12. el animal   _____
13. el volcán   _____

14. el pastor   _____
15. el motor   _____

Now, change the articles below from definite articles to indefinite articles and write the English equivalent. For example: *el sombrero—un sombrero; the hat—a hat; los chocolates—unos chocolates; the chocolates—some chocolates.*

16. el café   _____
17. los sofás   _____
18. la rosa   _____
19. el actor   _____
20. los carros   _____

In case you were wondering, *un* and *una* can also be used for the number one. *Un café* means "a coffee" and also "one coffee." *Una rosa* means "a rose" and also "one rose." It's a shortened version of the number one, *uno*.

Chapter 2

Here are some new nouns that are easy to understand because they resemble English: *carpintero, papá, fruta, profesor, violinista, posibilidad, religión, inventor, novelista, diferente, astronauta, moderno, misterioso, romántico, economista, aplicación, idealista, lenguaje.* Now, go back and look on pages 15–17 to find other nouns that will also be used in this next exercise and in exercises to follow. You may want to review these each time you start a new set of exercises.

Translate the following phrases into Spanish. (Pay close attention to the article!)

1. an elegant ballet   _____

2. the Mexican professor   _____

3. a fantastic father   _____

4. a different fruit   _____

5. a mysterious religion   _____

6. a fabulous carpenter   _____

7. an American violinist   _____

8. an excellent possibility   _____

9. the romantic novelists   _____

10. some important inventors   _____

11. an intelligent economist   _____

12. some interesting applications   _____

13. a positive person   _____

14. a special language   _____

15. some curious tourists   _____

Can you write some of your own phrases here, using the preceding vocabulary and from pages 15–17?

_____

_____

_____

Chapter 3

Translate the following into English. For example: *el chocolate de mi amiga—my (female) friend's chocolate.*

Note that feminine possessive is *de la*, but the masculine form is NOT *de el*. The masculine is *del*. This is a contraction of *de + el*. You can find a picture of *Del* in Chapter 17.

1. el carro de tu amigo _____

2. la blusa de mi mamá _____

3. las sandalias de mi papá _____

4. la hamburguesa de Pablo _____

5. las rosas de Carmen _____

6. los diccionarios de la secretaria _____

7. la guitarra de María _____

8. la bicicleta de José _____

9. el piano de la pianista _____

10. la computadora de la profesora _____

11. la flexibilidad del taxista _____

12. las emociones del motorista _____

Now, translate these phrases into Spanish (look at pages 15–17 for reference).

13. my guitar _____

14. his obligations _____

15. her interpretation _____

16. my imagination _____

17. your appetite _____

18. their problem _____

19. my radio _____

20. our decision (*see page 34*) _____

21. your condition _____

22. her education _____

Chapter 4

Translate these demonstrative phrases into English.

1. esa (aquella) bebida deliciosa _____

2. esta colección rara _____

3. estos actores románticos _____

4. esos (aquellos) volcanes activos _____

5. aquellas (esas) estructuras modernas _____

6. esa (aquella) acción ilegal _____

7. estas excursiones especiales _____

Now, translate the following phrases into Spanish. For example: *this popular restaurant—este restaurante popular.* (Be sure to look up new words on pages 15–17.)

8. that classic car _____

9. this ideal community _____

10. that fantastic guitarist _____

11. this intelligent animal _____

12. these superior carpenters _____

13. those fabulous computers _____

14. these rapid (fast) bicycles _____

Chapters 5 and 6

Translate the following sentences into English.

1. El astronauta explora el espacio.

   _____

2. Nosotros celebramos este momento importante.

   _____

3. Yo comprendo español (*Spanish*).

   _____

4. Nosotros vendemos calendarios.

   _____

5. ¿Tú comprendes ese lenguaje misterioso?

   _____

Now, can you translate these sentences into Spanish?

6. We divide the portions.

   _____

7. They sell computers.

   _____

8. I order a hamburger in the restaurant. (in = *en*)

   _____

9. The girls wash themselves in the house.

   _____

10. The girls are called (are named) Margarita and Rosita.

    _____

Chapter 7

Translate the following questions or negative statements into English.

1. Nunca estudio en mi casa. (*en* = in)

   _____

2. ¡Nosotros no plantamos tomates en las montañas!

   _____

3. ¿Cómo se llama tu mamá?

   _____

4. ¡Los fatalistas nunca usan su imaginación!

   _____

5. Ella no comprende inglés (*English*).

   _____

Now, can you translate these English questions or negative sentences into Spanish?

6. When are you selling (do you sell) your car?

   _____

7. Does the teacher answer in English or Spanish?

   _____

8. Nobody studies in my house.

   _____

9. Do you understand English?

   _____

10. She never orders tacos in a Spanish restaurant.

    _____

Chapters 8 and 9

Now that you understand the two major "to be" verbs, fill in the blanks with the correct form of *ser* or *estar*.

1. Yo _____ en el restaurante.

2. José _____ artista.

3. Los elefantes _____ en el zoo.

4. San Francisco _____ en California.

5. Nosotros _____ inteligentes.

6. ¿Tú _____ frustrada?

7. Estos carpinteros _____ excelentes.

8. Ellos _____ contentos.

9. Yo _____ americana.

10. ¿Tú _____ mexicana?

Fill in the blanks with a **-go** verb. Choose from the following.

tengo = I have   **vengo** = I come   **oigo** = I hear
digo = I say   **pongo** = I put   **salgo** = I leave/go out
hago = I make/do   **traigo** = I bring   **caigo** = I fall

11. _____ a la clase. (*I come*)

12. _____ mi libro. (*I bring*)

13. _____ un CD. (*I have*)

14. _____ el CD en el estéreo. (*I put*)

15. _____ la música. (*I hear*)

16. _____ aerobic. (*I do*)

17. ¡_____! (*I fall!*)

18. _____ "¡Ay!" (*I say "Ouch!"*)

19. _____ (*I leave/go out*)

This is a very useful sequence to help you memorize the nine -**go** verbs in Spanish. Pantomime the nine actions several times and say each sentence as you do the action. From now on, you will always know the nine -**go** verbs!

Chapter 11

Here are a few fun new verbs that will help you do the exercises that follow: *prestar* (to loan), *abrazar* (to embrace/to hug), *besar* (to kiss). Notice that the word *a* appears after the verbs "hug" and "kiss." This is a "ghost preposition." Look in Chapter 17 to find a picture and explanation of this ghost preposition!

Translate the following sentences into English.

1. Yo abrazo a Juan. Yo lo abrazo.

   _____

2. Juan besa a María. Juan la besa.

   _____

3. Usted pasa el libro a Rosita. Usted se lo pasa.

   _____

4. Nosotros damos los chocolates a mamá. Nosotros se los damos.

   _____

5. Tú escribes a Antonia. Tú le escribes.

   _____

Fill in the blank with the correct DOP or IOP, or, in some cases, the double DOP/IOP.

6. Carmelita presta $10 a Pepe. Carmelita _____ presta $10.

7. Juan presta $20 a nosotros. Juan _____ presta $20.

8. Juanita escribe un e-mail a José. Ella _____ escribe a José.

9. José escribe un e-mail a ella. Él _____ escribe un e-mail.

10. Ella escribe un e-mail a José. Ella _____ escribe.

Chapter 12

Translate the following sentences into Spanish using regular preterite verbs.

1. They ordered pizza in the Italian restaurant.

_____

2. I transported my bicycle to California.

_____

3. The tourists explored the ruins in Peru.

_____

4. Did you understand the conversation in Spanish? (_Use_ tú.)

_____

5. I invited my mom to my house. (_Use ghost preposition_ a.)

_____

Translate the following sentences into English using the irregular preterite forms.

6. Helena vino a mi casa para (_to_) admirar mi jardín.

_____

7. Puse el sandwich en el piano.

_____

8. ¡Tuve un accidente horrible!

_____

Now, based on the previous exercise, translate these sentences to Spanish. You can look in the Appendix for the complete irregular preterite conjugations.

9. I went to the American university in Venezuela.

_____

10. Juan and Pepe came to my party.

_____

Chapter 13

Translate the following first-person story into English. It tells about the childhood of a little girl in Mexico. Here is some new vocabulary that will help you. These new words are italicized in the story.

la niña = little girl	**vivir** = to live	**chiquito** = very tiny
trabajar = to work	**y** = and	**de** = from
la escuela = school	**enfrente de** = in front of	**el dinero** = money
pero = but	**los hermanos** = brothers and sisters	**la calle** = street
los abuelos = grandparents	**siempre** = always	**reparar** = to repair
los televisores = television sets	**muy grande** = very big	**la tele** = T.V.
los sábados = on Saturday	**con** = with	**el queso** = cheese
diciembre = December	**otros** = other	

Cuando yo era *niña*, *vivía* en un pueblo muy *chiquito*. Mi papá era guitarrista en un restaurante. Mi mamá *trabajaba* en la casa, *y* vendía chocolates a los muchachos que venían *de la escuela* y pasaban *enfrente de* nuestra casa. No teníamos mucho *dinero*, *pero* teníamos muchas rosas en nuestro jardín, y mis *hermanos* y yo vendíamos rosas en *la calle*.

Cuando mi mamá no estaba en casa, íbamos a la casa de mis *abuelos*. Mi abuela *siempre* nos daba helado de vainilla. Mi abuelo *reparaba televisores*, y mis abuelos tenían un televisor *muy grande*. Me gustaba ver *la tele* en su casa.

Los sábados, íbamos *con* toda la familia a un restaurante. Me gustaba ordenar enchiladas de *queso* y limonada. En *diciembre*, visitábamos a mis *otros* abuelos en la capital, y celebrábamos la Navidad *con* ellos.

Chapter 14

Go back to the sentences on page 116 and write in the real future tense of each verb, adding the subject pronoun. Watch out! Some of the verbs in this new exercise have been changed to a different person.

Example: *Voy a invitar a Carlos a mi casa.—Yo invitaré a Carlos a mi casa.*

1. Voy a depositar pesos mexicanos en el banco.

   _____

2. Vamos a plantar flores en el jardín.

   _____

3. Van a pasar enfrente de la farmacia.

   _____

4. ¡Vas a inventar chocolate sin calorías!

   _____

5. Voy a comunicarme con papá.

   Yo me _____

6. Vamos a llamar a mi mamá.

   _____

7. Juanita va a usar un cheque en el restaurante.

   _____

8. Voy a ir a la casa de Miguel.

   _____

9. Ellos van a ser astronautas.

   _____

10. Vamos a estar en el hotel a las 10 de la mañana (*in the morning*).

   _____

Chapter 15

Now, let's practice some "if . . . then" sentences in Spanish! Here are the same sentences from Chapter 14. Rewrite them using the conditional endings and adding *si* (if) at the end of each sentence.

Example: *Yo invitaré a Carlos a mi casa.*—*Yo invitaría a Carlos a mi casa si...* (I would invite Carlos to my house if . . .)

1. Yo depositaré pesos mexicanos en el banco.

   _____

2. Nosotros plantaremos flores en el jardín.

   _____

3. Ellos pasarán enfrente de la farmacia.

   _____

4. ¡Tú inventarás chocolate sin calorías!

   _____

5. Me comunicaré con papá.

   _____

6. Llamaremos a mi mamá.

   _____

7. Juanita usará un cheque en el restaurante.

   _____

8. Yo iré a la casa de Miguel.

   _____

9. Ellos serán astronautas.

   _____

10. Nosotros estaremos en el hotel a las 10 de la mañana.

    _____

Chapter 16

Now, let's play Alibi in reverse! You are the bilingual interpreter for an American detective at the police station, as well as for each of the five English-speaking suspects. Who is innocent and who is guilty? First use the imperfect.

DETECTIVE: Where were you, and who were you with on the night of the crime?

YOU: ¿————————————————— la noche del crimen?

SUSPECT #1: I was in a restaurant with my brothers and sisters.

YOU: —————————————————————.

SUSPECT #2: I was in the garden with my pastor.

YOU: —————————————————————.

SUSPECT #3: I was at the zoo with the elephants.

YOU: —————————————————————.

SUSPECT #4: I was at my apartment. I wasn't with anyone.

YOU: —————————————————————.

SUSPECT #5: I was at the hospital with my grandmother.

YOU: —————————————————————.

Now use the progressive imperfect (e.g. *yo estaba estudiando*).

DETECTIVE: What were you doing on the night of the crime?

YOU: ¿————————————— la noche del crimen? (verb: *hacer*)

SUSPECT #1: We were selling roses.

YOU: —————————————————————.

SUSPECT #2: We were planting tomatoes.

YOU: —————————————————————.

SUSPECT #3: We were writing e-mails on the computer.

YOU: —————————————————————.

SUSPECT #4: I was repairing my TV set.

YOU: —————————————————————.

SUSPECT #5: We were painting.

YOU: —————————————————————.

Chapter 17

Translate the following sentences into Spanish, using prepositions and conjunctions.

1. She is going *to* the pharmacy.

   _____

2. I prefer coffee *without* sugar (*azúcar*).

   _____

3. This taco is *for* my friend Hector. (note: do not use *por*)

   _____

4. He watched (observed) the snow *through* the window.

   _____

5. Victoria is *from* Guatemala.

   _____

6. I understand Spanish *but* I don't speak (*hablar*) it.

   _____

Translate the following sentences into Spanish using GHOST prepositions and conjunctions.

7. We visited my grandfather in the hospital.

   _____

8. I think Spanish is an interesting language. (language = *idioma*)

   _____

9. The criminals insist (*insistir en que*) they are innocent.

   _____

10. Do you think this activity is difficult (*difícil*)?

   _____

Chapter 18

Go back and review the *-go* verbs on page 84. The command, or imperative form of the *-go* verbs is formed by changing the first person *-o* ending to *-a*. Can you fill in the rest of the table below?

Present indicative	Imperative singular	Imperative plural	English
Vengo	¡Venga!	¡Vengan!	Come!
Tengo	_____	_____	_____
Traigo	_____	_____	_____
Pongo	_____	_____	_____
Oigo	_____	_____	_____
Hago	_____	_____	_____
Caigo	_____	_____	_____
Digo	_____	_____	_____
Salgo	_____	_____	_____

Now, can you translate these sentences?

1. ¡Haga los ejercicios!

   _____

2. ¡Tráigame el libro!

   _____

3. ¡No digan eso!

   _____

4. ¡Oiga la música!

   _____

5. ¡Vengan a mi fiesta!

   _____

Chapter 19

Translate these sentences into Spanish.

1. What have you bought?

_____

2. Have you been to Mexico?

_____

3. They have not studied Spanish.

_____

4. We had not understood the exercises.

_____

5. My grandfather has repaired many (*muchos*) television sets.

_____

6. They have lived in Colombia for (*por*) ten years (*años*).

_____

7. My mother had planted roses in her garden.

_____

8. She has invited her grandparents to her house for (*para*) Christmas.

_____

9. Have you (*tú*) eaten banana (*plátano*) and chocolate sandwiches?

_____

10. Have you sold the house?

_____

Chapter 20

Can you translate these sentences into English?

1. Ojalá que Santa Claus me traiga una guitarra.

   _____

2. Es importante que tú hables en español.

   _____

3. Es necesario que yo escriba correctamente.

   _____

4. Esperamos que tengas una feliz Navidad.

   _____

5. Es importante que estudien en la clase.

   _____

Now, can you translate these wishes into Spanish?

6. I want you to buy (*comprar*) me a sandwich.

   _____

7. It's important that you bring your book to class (*la clase*).

   _____

8. I hope you write me an e-mail.

   _____

9. It's possible that he works at the university.

   _____

10. It's necessary for you to eat a lot of fruit!

    _____

Answers to Extra Credit Exercises

Chapter 1

1. las bananas
2. los patos
3. los apartamentos
4. las ranas
5. los gatos
6. los sofás
7. las muchachas
8. los sombreros
9. las niñas
10. los carros
11. los actores
12. los animales
13. los volcanes (no accent is needed on plurals of nouns ending in -n)
14. los pastores
15. los motores
16. un café, the coffee, a coffee
17. unos sofás, the sofas, some sofas
18. una rosa, the rose, a rose
19. un actor, the actor, an actor
20. unos carros, the cars, some cars

Chapter 2

1. un ballet elegante
2. el profesor mexicano (nationalities, languages, days of the week, months are not capitalized in Spanish)
3. un papá fantástico
4. una fruta diferente
5. una religión misteriosa
6. un carpintero fabuloso
7. un violinista americano
8. una posibilidad excelente
9. los novelistas románticos
10. unos inventores importantes
11. un economista inteligente
12. unas aplicaciones interesantes
13. una persona positiva
14. un lenguaje especial
15. unos turistas curiosos

Chapter 3

1. your friend's car
2. my mom's blouse
3. my dad's sandals
4. Pablo's hamburger
5. Carmen's roses
6. the secretary's dictionaries
7. María's guitar
8. José's bicycle
9. the pianist's piano
10. the teacher's computer
11. the taxi driver's flexibility
12. the motorist's emotions
13. mi guitarra
14. sus obligaciones
15. su interpretación
16. mi imaginación
17. su (tu) apetito
18. su problema
19. mi radio
20. nuestra decisión
21. su (tu) condición
22. su educación

Chapter 4

1. that delicious drink
2. this rare collection
3. these romantic actors
4. those active volcanoes
5. those modern structures
6. that illegal action
7. these special excursions
8. ese (aquel) carro clásico
9. esta comunidad ideal
10. ese (aquel) guitarrista fantástico
11. este animal inteligente
12. estos carpinteros superiores
13. esas (aquellas) computadoras fabulosas
14. estas bicicletas rápidas

Chapters 5 and 6

1. The astronaut explores space.
2. We celebrate this important moment.
3. I understand Spanish.
4. We sell calendars.
5. Do you understand that mysterious language?
6. Nosotros dividimos las porciones.
7. Ellos venden computadoras.
8. Yo ordeno una hamburguesa en el restaurante.
9. Las muchachas se lavan en la casa.
10. Las muchachas se llaman Margarita y Rosita.

Chapter 7

1. I never study in my house.
2. We don't plant tomatoes in the mountains!
3. What's your mother's name? (How does your mother call herself?)
4. Fatalists never use their imagination!
5. She doesn't understand English.
6. ¿Cuándo vende(s) su (tu) carro?
7. ¿El profesor responde en inglés o en español?
8. Nadie estudia en mi casa. (*or:* No estudia nadie en mi casa.)
9. ¿Usted comprende inglés? (¿Tú comprendes inglés?)
10. Ella nunca ordena tacos en un restaurante español.

Chapters 8 and 9

1. estoy
2. es
3. están
4. está
5. somos
6. estás
7. son
8. están
9. soy
10. eres
11. Vengo
12. Traigo
13. Tengo
14. Pongo
15. Oigo
16. Hago
17. Caigo
18. Digo
19. Salgo

Chapter 11

1. I hug John. I hug him.
2. Juan kisses María. Juan kisses her.
3. You pass the book to Rosita. You pass it to her.
4. We give the chocolates to Mom. We give them to her.
5. You write to Antonia. You write to her.
6. le
7. nos
8. lo
9. le
10. lo

Chapter 12

1. Ellos ordenaron pizza en el restaurante italiano.
2. Yo transporté mi bicicleta a California.
3. Los turistas exploraron las ruinas en el Perú.
4. ¿Tú comprendiste (entendiste) la conversación en español?
5. Invité a mi mamá a mi casa.
6. Helena came to my house to admire my garden.
7. I put the sandwich on the piano.
8. I had a horrible accident!
9. Fui a la universidad americana en Venezuela.
10. Juan y Pepe vinieron a mi fiesta.

Chapter 13

When I was a little girl, I lived in a very tiny town. My father was a guitarist in a restaurant. My mother used to work at home, and sold chocolates to children who were coming from school and passed in front of our house. We didn't have a lot of money, but we had a lot of roses in our garden, so my brothers and sisters and I sold roses in the street.

When my mother wasn't at home, we used to go to my grandparents' house. My grandmother always gave us vanilla ice cream. My grandfather repaired television sets, and my grandparents had a very big television. I liked to watch TV at their house.

On Saturdays, we used to go with the whole family to a restaurant. I liked to order cheese enchiladas and lemonade. In December, we used to visit my other grandparents in the capital, and we used to celebrate Christmas with them.

Chapter 14

1. Yo depositaré pesos mexicanos en el banco.
2. Nosotros plantaremos flores en el jardín.
3. Ellos pasarán enfrente de la farmacia.
4. ¡Tú inventarás chocolate sin calorías!
5. Me comunicaré con papá.
6. Llamaremos a mi mamá.
7. Juanita usará un cheque en el restaurante.
8. Yo iré a la casa de Miguel.
9. Ellos serán astronautas.
10. Nosotros estaremos en el hotel a las 10 de la mañana.

Chapter 15

1. Yo depositaría pesos mexicanos en el banco si...
2. Nosotros plantaríamos flores en el jardín si...
3. Ellos pasarían enfrente de la farmacia si...
4. ¡Tú inventarías chocolate sin calorías si...!
5. Me comunicaría con papá si...
6. Llamaríamos a mi mamá si...
7. Juanita usaría un cheque en el restaurante si...
8. Yo iría a la casa de Miguel si...
9. Ellos serían astronautas si...
10. Nosotros estaríamos en el hotel a las 10 de la mañana si...

Chapter 16

¿Dónde estaba y con quién estaba, la noche del crimen?
#1: Yo estaba en un restaurante con mis hermanos.
#2: Yo estaba en el jardín con mi pastor.
#3: Yo estaba en el zoo con los elefantes.
#4: Yo estaba en mi apartamento. No estaba con nadie.
#5: Yo estaba en el hospital con mi abuela.

¿Qué estaba haciendo la noche del crimen?
#1: Estábamos vendiendo rosas.
#2: Estábamos plantando tomates.
#3: Estábamos escribiendo e-mails en la computadora.
#4: Estaba reparando mi televisor.
#5: Estábamos pintando.

Did you figure out who is the guilty one? Number 3!

Chapter 17

1. Ella va a la farmacia.
2. Yo prefiero el café sin azúcar.
3. Este taco es para mi amigo Hector.
4. Él observó la nieve por la ventana.
5. Victoria es de Guatemala.
6. Yo comprendo/entiendo español, pero no lo hablo.
7. Nosotros visitamos a mi abuelo en el hospital.
8. Yo pienso que el español es un idioma interesante.
9. Los criminales insistir en que ellos son inocentes.
10. ¿Piensa usted que esta actividad es difícil?

Chapter 18

Tengo	¡Tenga!	¡Tengan!	Have!
Traigo	¡Traiga!	¡Traigan!	Bring!
Pongo	¡Ponga!	¡Pongan!	Put!
Oigo	¡Oiga!	¡Oigan!	Listen! (hear)
Hago	¡Haga!	¡Hagan!	Make/do!
Caigo	¡Caiga!	¡Caigan!	Fall!
Digo	¡Diga!	¡Digan!	Say!
Salgo	¡Salga!	¡Salgan!	Leave!

1. Do the exercises!
2. Bring me the book!
3. Don't say that!
4. Listen to (hear) the music!
5. Come to my party!

Chapter 19

1. ¿Qué ha (has) comprado?
2. ¿Ha (has) estado en México?
3. Ellos no han estudiado español.
4. No habíamos comprendido los ejercicios.
5. Mi abuelo ha reparado muchos televisores.
6. Han vivido en Colombia por 10 años.
7. Mi mamá había plantado rosas en su jardín.
8. Ella ha invitado a sus abuelos a su casa para la Navidad.
9. ¿Has comido sandwiches de plátano y chocolate?
10. ¿Ha (has) vendido la casa?

Chapter 20

1. I hope Santa Claus brings me a guitar.
2. It's important that you speak in Spanish.
3. It's necessary that I write correctly.
4. We hope that you have a Merry Christmas.
5. It's important that you (they) study in the class.
6. Quiero que me compre (compres) un sandwich.
7. Es importante que traiga (traigas) su (tu) libro a la clase.
8. Espero que me escriba (escribas) un e-mail.
9. Es posible que él trabaje en la universidad.
10. Es necesario que usted (tú) coma (comas) mucha fruta!

Glossary

Abear The verb *haber* (to have) is used primarily with past participle verbs to form a compound tense. I have visited, *he visitado*. (Chapter 19)

Accents Used so you emphasize or stress a sound or syllable. See "Squashed Bugs." (Section One, Part Five)

Adjective A word that tells you more about a noun. Red, tall, old (descriptive adjectives), my (possessive adjective), this (demonstrative adjective). (Chapters 2, 3, 4)

Adverb A word that tells you more about a verb, often ending in *-ly* (English), or *-mente* (Spanish). Sincerely, *sinceramente*. (Chapter 10)

Agreement Used with adjectives. An adjective agrees with the noun it describes, like a chameleon. See "About Chameleons." (Chapter 2)

A kel Written *aquel*, demonstrative adjective meaning "that over there." Also *aquella (f.), aquellos, aquellas*, those over there. (Chapter 4)

Apostrophe s In Spanish there is no apostrophe s to show something belongs to you. John's chocolate = *el chocolate de Juan*. (Chapter 3)

Articles Those little words that mean "the" in Spanish: *la, el, las, los* (definite articles); or "a/an" or "some": *una, un, unas, unos* (indefinite articles). Spanish nouns almost always have an article before them. (Chapter 1)

Auxiliary verbs Verbs that help in the conjugation of another verb. He has explored, I have gone: require *haber* in Spanish (Abear). I'm running, she's reading: require *estar* in Spanish. (Chapters 16, 19)

Boomerang verbs To wash yourself, dress yourself. See the discussion on reflexive verbs. (Chapter 6)

'Burbs See verbs. *B*s and *v*s sound the same in Spanish! (Chapter 6)

Chameleons Descriptive adjectives change in gender and number like a chameleon to match the noun they describe. Houses bigs, *casas grandes*. (Chapter 2)

Clauses Dependent clause = a group of words that has a subject and verb but does not form a complete sentence. Example: If I won the lottery. Independent clause = a group of words that does form a complete sentence. Example: I would buy a yacht. (Chapter 15)

Cognates Words that look like English in another language. There are over 4,000 Spanish cognates. *Presidente, dentista, superior, explorar*. (Section One, Part Six)

Command verbs See the discussion on imperative mood. Come here! Sit down! Eat your spinach! (Chapter 18)

Comparatives A form of an adjective or adverb that tells you if something is more or less. Bigger, less big. *Más grande, menos grande*. (Chapter 10)

Compound tenses Composed of two verbs, such as "have" + a past participle in Spanish (*haber*; see "The Story of Abear") + a present participle. (Chapter 19)

Conditional tense A verb in future time telling what you "would" do. Usually needs an "if" clause. I would explore, *yo exploraría*. (Chapter 15)

Conjugate   To say or list a verb with all the personal pronouns. In Spanish, conjugated verbs have different endings. *Uso, usas, usa*, etc. (Chapter 6)

Conjugated verb   Any verb that has a subject. The only verbs not conjugated are infinitives and participles. I explore, *yo exploro*. (Chapter 6)

Conjunctions   Little words that link words, phrases, clauses, or sentences. Or, and, if, but, that (*o, y, si, pero, que*). See "The Ghost Conjunction." (Chapter 17)

Consonants   Any letter of the alphabet that is not a vowel: *b, c, d, x, z*, etc. (Section One, Part One)

Demonstratives   Hugging and kissing words. Adjectives or pronouns that point out an item. This, that, these, those. *Este, ese, estos, esos.* (Chapter 4)

Descriptive adjective   A word that describes a noun. Tall, blue. In Spanish, descriptive adjectives follow the noun. Tree tall, shirt blue. (Chapter 2)

Diminutives   Honey, I shrunk the world! Making words smaller in meaning by adding an ending. Little car, little Grandma. *Carrito, Abuelita.* (Chapter 13)

Diphthongs   Bathing suits or sandals? No! Combinations of two vowels. In Spanish, *ua, ue, io, au, oi,* etc. (Section One, Part Four)

Direct object pronoun   See "DOPs." (Chapter 11)

DOPs   Direct object pronouns, answer the question "who?" "what?" I see it. *Me, te, lo/la, nos, los/las.* (Chapter 11)

Endings/beginnings   Parts of a verb. Endings: *-ar, -er,* and *-ir* (for the infinitives) and the different endings you add to conjugate them. Beginnings are called the root or stem. (Chapter 6)

Exclamations   Express emotions. In Spanish, you always write an upside-down exclamation point before an exclamation. Wow! *¡Caramba!* (Chapter 7)

Extra letters   There is one extra letter in the Spanish alphabet: ñ: *mañana.* The consonant blends *rr, ll, ch* are like extra letters because they represent single sounds: *carro, llama, muchacho.* (Section One, Part Four)

Future tense   Verbs that tell you an action that will happen in the future. Made of two verbs (compound) in English, one in Spanish. I will be, *seré.* (Chapter 14)

Gender   All about sex, the birds and the bees. All nouns in Spanish have a gender: masculine or feminine. Nouns often end in *-o* for masculine, *-a* for feminine (Chapter 1)

Ghost conjunction   *Que* (that), often not seen or heard in English, but always needed in Spanish. I know (that) my cat has fleas. (Chapter 17)

Ghost preposition   "The personal *a*," invisible in English. Used when the direct object is a person. I visit Mary. *Visito a María.* (Chapter 17)

-Go verbs   End in *-go* in the first-person present. You can draw a flower around them. *Tengo, vengo, salgo, digo, pongo,* etc. (Chapter 9)

Hay   *¡Ay, ay, ay!* Means "there is" or "there are." *Hay insectos grandes en el garaje.* There are large insects in the garage. (Chapter 19)

Imperative mood   The emperor commands, so it's the command form. It's a mood and you can't plot it on a time line. Come here! Sit down! (Chapter 18)

Imperfect tense   Used for an action in the past that was not perfectly past or completed. I used to admire, I was receiving. *Admiraba, recibía.* (Chapter 13)

Indicative   One of three verb moods (with subjunctive and imperative). Indicative tenses include present, preterite, imperfect, pluperfect, and future. (Chapter 6)

Indirect object pronoun   See "IOPs." (Chapter 11)

Infinitive verbs Unconjugated verbs. To be, to explore, to sell. *Ser, estar, explorar, vender.* End in *-ar, -er, -ir* in Spanish. (Chapter 6)

-Ing verbs Present progressive tense. Used with *estar* in Spanish. Endings: *-ando, -iendo.* I am exploring, *estoy explorando.* I am selling, *estoy vendiendo.* (Chapter 16)

Interrogatives Question words or sentences. How, when, where, why, what? *¿Cómo, cuándo, dónde, por qué, qué?* Preceded by the upside-down question mark. (Chapter 7)

IOPs Indirect object pronouns, answering the question "to whom?" or "to what?" Give the ball to me. *Me, te, le, nos, les.* (Chapter 11)

Irregular verbs Verbs that don't follow the rules, or that deviate from the pattern, when they are conjugated. *Ser = soy, eres, es, somos, son.* (Chapter 9)

Me too, Sue! Possessive adjectives. Placed before the noun. *Mi chocolate, tu carro, su elefante.* Plural: *mis, tus, sus.* (Chapter 3)

Moods There are three moods in Spanish: indicative, imperative, and subjunctive. Only the indicative can be put on a time line. (Chapters 6, 18, 20)

Negatives Words that deny the affirmative or positive. In Spanish use *no*: "He no goes"; *él no va.* Negative words: *no, nunca, nadie* (not, never, no one). (Chapter 7)

Noun A word that names a person, place, thing, or abstraction. John, town, hat, love. *Juan, pueblo, sombrero, amor.* Article is required! (Chapter 1)

Number Refers to whether there is one or more than one (singular or plural). Boy, house, boys, houses. *Muchacho, casa, muchachos, casas.* (Chapter 1)

Object Noun or pronoun that receives the action of the verb. There are direct and indirect objects. See "DOPs" and "IOPs." (Chapter 11)

Object pronouns See "DOPs" and "IOPs." (Chapter 11)

Past participles Verb forms like flown, eaten (in English), *explorado, recibido* (ending in *-do* in Spanish). Used with *haber* (to have). (Chapter 19)

Past tense A verb where the action has already happened. Preterite or imperfect, in Spanish. I used, used to use. *Usé, usaba.* (Chapters 12, 13)

Perfect tense A verb that is very past—it is done and finished. See the discussion on compound tenses. (Chapter 19)

Person The form of the pronoun and the verb you are referring to. There are three persons in the singular: first person (I), second person (you), third person (he, she, it); and three persons in the plural: first person (we), second person (you all), third person (they). In Spanish the formal pronouns *usted/ustedes* (you/you all) are considered third person. (Chapter 5)

Personal pronouns The ones doing the action. I, you, he, she, it, we, you, they. *Yo, tú, él, ella, usted, nosotros, ellos, ellas, ustedes.* (Chapter 5)

Pluperfect tense More perfect than perfect, more past than past. I had explored. *Había explorado.* Use the imperfect of *haber.* See "The Story of Abear." (Chapter 19)

Plural The opposite of singular. More than one. Refers to number of nouns, adjectives, or pronouns. Lemonades, cold, they. (Chapter 1)

Possessive People who won't share! Refers to ownership. Possessive adjectives: my toy, your house, his car. See "Me Too, Sue!" (Chapter 3)

Prepositional phrase A group of words that contains a preposition and an object of a preposition. With my mom, at the beach, in the car. (Chapter 17)

Prepositions Little words, like bonbons or candy. To, from, on, in, for, with, without. *A, de, en, por, para, con, sin.* ("Twinkle, Twinkle, Little Star.") (Chapter 17)

Present progressive   A verb tense where the action is continuing. See "-ing" verbs. (Chapter 16)

Present tense   Can be plotted on a time line. I admire, I receive. *Admiro, recibo.* (Chapter 6)

Preterite tense   Past tense verbs that can be plotted on a time line, completely finished in the past. I came, I saw, I conquered. (Chapter 12)

Pronouns   Words that replace a noun. He (Pablo), she (Carmen), it (the rose). To me, to them. See the discussion on personal pronouns and "DOPs" and "IOPs." (Chapters 5, 11)

Proper nouns   Words that name a person or place. Carlos, Argentina, San Juan. (Chapter 1)

Question words   How, when, where, why, what? See the discussion on interrogatives. (Chapter 7)

Reflexive pronoun   A pronoun that refers to the same person as the subject. Myself, yourself, himself. *Me, te, se.* Goes with "boomerang verbs." (Chapter 6)

Reflexive verbs   Boomerang verbs. Where the action comes back to the subject. I wash myself. She dresses herself. (Chapter 6)

Ser* and *estar   The main "to be" verbs in Spanish. *Ser* is used for permanent attributes (tall, farmer). *Estar* is for location, *-ing* verbs, health. (Chapter 8)

Sex   Masculine or feminine. See the discussion on gender. (Chapter 1)

Singular   Used with single objects or persons. Boy, house. The opposite is plural. See the discussion on number. (Chapter 1)

Squashed bugs   Accent marks in Spanish. Used to emphasize or stress a sound or syllable. *Papá. Mamá.* (Section One, Part Five)

Stem or root   Main part of the verb without the *-ar, -er,* or *-ir. Observ(ar), vend(er), recib(ir).* (Chapters 6, 9)

Stem-changing verb   Verb where the stem changes to different letters in all persons except *nosotros. e–ie (entender–entiende)* and *o–ue (costar–cuesta).* (Chapter 9)

Subject   Who did it? The person/thing responsible for the action in a clause/sentence. The astronaut explored. *El astronauta exploró.* (Chapter 5)

Subjunctive mood   Like wishing on a star, verbs can't be put on a time line. Expresses doubt, uncertainty. *A* becomes *e, e* becomes *a.* (Chapter 20)

Superlative   Form of the adjective or adverb that shows "the most" or "the least" amount. Biggest, smallest. *El más grande, el más chico.* (Chapter 10)

Syllable   The way to divide a word so it's easy to pronounce. Simple ones are made from a consonant and a vowel (*fa-mo-so*). (Section One, Part Six)

Tenses   Tell you when in time the action of a verb takes place, usually present, past, future. There are lots of tenses in Spanish. (Chapters 6, 12–16, 19)

Tilde   A "squashed bug." Looks like this ~ and goes over the letter *n* in Spanish. *Mañana, piña.* (Section One, Part Five)

Tú* and *usted   You. *Tú* = informal, used with a best friend, a baby, your relatives. *Usted (Ud.)* = formal, polite, used to show respect. (Chapter 5)

Verbs ('burbs)   Actions that go hand in hand with people, with personal or subject pronouns. I AM, you EAT, he RUNS. (Chapter 6)

Vowels (bowels)   A, E, I, O, U (Y) in Spanish. The opposite of consonants. (Section One, Part One)

About the Author

Arlene M. Jullie was born in São Paulo, Brazil, of American missionary parents. She lived and attended schools in Brazil until coming to the United States as a high school senior. She received her B.A. in Spanish and French from Hanover College, studied and taught French in Neuchâtel, Switzerland, and holds an M.A. in French Literature from Emory University. She has done graduate work at the University of Minnesota in Spanish Literature and has taught languages for more than 25 years. She is the author of the *EasyLearn* tapes in Spanish and French.

Jullie is fluent in six languages: Spanish, Portuguese, French, Italian, English, and German. She is the founder and president of International Language Services, Inc., a language translation company in Minneapolis, Minnesota.